Traditional Teatime Recipes

Traditional Teatime Recipes

Jane Pettigrew

NATIONAL TRUST BOOKS

The third edition of this book has been made possible through a great deal of hard work, planning and editing by the team at Anova Books and Home Economist Jane Suthering, and wonderful photography from Tara Fisher. The re-publication of this collection of National Trust recipes is a sign, I feel, of the continuing and perhaps increasing popularity of tea and teatime in Britain.

First published in Great Britain in 1991 by
National Trust Enterprises Limited
Reprinted 1992,1993 and 1995
Revised edition published in Great Britain in 2001 by
National Trust Enterprises Limited

This edition published in the United Kingdom in 2007 by
National Trust Books
10 Southcombe Street
London W14 0RA

An imprint of Anova Books Ltd

ISBN-13 9781905400522

A CIP catalogue record for this book is available from the British Library.

15 14 13 12 11 10 09 08 07
10 9 8 7 6 5 4 3 2 1

Reproduction by Spectrum Colour Ltd, England
Printed and bound by CT Printing Ltd, China

Design by Lee-May Lim
Photography by Tara Fisher
Home Economy by Jane Suthering

This book can be ordered direct from the publisher at the website: www.anovabooks.com, or try your local bookshop. Also available at National Trust shops.

Contents

6

Introduction

In the early days of the National Trust, visitors to the properties were sometimes offered a cup of tea and a bun at the kitchen door or in some suitable corner of the house or garden. Nowadays, many properties provide morning coffee, lunches, afternoon teas and, sometimes, evening meals or special functions in prestigious and stylish restaurants. The food is always of a high standard, and in many areas local people make special trips just to have lunch or tea at their nearby National Trust house or garden.

By sitting down to enjoy a cup of tea and a sandwich or a piece of cake, National Trust visitors are perpetuating a ritual that has its origins in Britain in the mid-17th century when tea started to arrive via Holland and Portugal, which had established trade routes to Japan and China a hundred years earlier. Merchants and aristocrats imported small amounts of tea into Britain in the 1650s, but it was Charles II's marriage in 1662 to a Portuguese princess, Catherine of Braganza, that established tea drinking as an accepted practice. Catherine brought to London a 3lb chest of tea as part of her dowry and she quickly introduced this to her friends at court. Regular consignments were soon being ordered for the King and Queen and tea drinking became a fashionable activity. Meanwhile enterprising merchants, keen to increase sales of this new commodity, engaged in elaborate advertising campaigns, and gradually the trend spread. Tea was served, and loose tea sold, in the coffee houses that had sprung up in London and some provincial towns in the 1650s, but the high tax levied by Charles II meant that it was very expensive and therefore out of the reach of the working classes. Ale and gin continued to be the standard drinks of the majority of the population until 1784, when the tax was reduced from 119 per cent to 12 per cent (to 2½d. per lb) and tea overtook gin and ale in the popularity stakes. Had the tax remained, it is likely that the British would have ended up drinking coffee like the French and Germans.

In the first half of the 18th century a powerful campaign against the coffee houses, which had become bawdy dens of iniquity, succeeded in closing them down, and, in their place, the pleasure gardens at Vauxhall, Chelsea, Marylebone, Islington,

Bermondsey, Kentish Town and Kilburn provided family entertainment in London. The price of entry to these gardens sometimes included tea with bread and butter, the idea being that, after enjoying rides on the river, horse-riding, listening to music or wandering through beautifully tended gardens, the family could relax and take some refreshment together. Sadly, the gardens survived for only a short time; by 1850 most had closed, but not before the ritual of afternoon tea had been firmly established as part of the British way of life. It is said to have been 'invented' in the early 19th century by Anna, wife of the 7th Duke of Bedford. Breakfast in those days was taken at nine or ten o'clock in the morning, and dinner, which had previously been eaten at two or three o'clock in the afternoon, was not until eight or nine o'clock. By four o'clock the Duchess, and no doubt others too, felt a little peckish; she therefore asked her footman to bring her all her tea-making equipage to her private room so that she could brew herself a pot of tea and enjoy it with a little light refreshment. The Duchess was so pleased with this arrangement that she started inviting her friends to join her, and soon all of London's elegant society was sipping 'afternoon tea' and gossiping all the while about people, places and events. With their tea they nibbled dainty sandwiches or neat slices of light sponge cake flavoured with candied orange or lemon peel, or caraway seeds. As the custom of taking tea became more popular, so the demand for teaware grew, and the potteries, silversmiths and furniture makers produced a wide range of tea services, cake plates, teaspoons, knives, strainers, teapots and kettles, caddies, caddy spoons and tea tables.

In 1884 the activities of the manageress of the London Bridge branch of the Aerated Bread Company (the ABC) brought afternoon tea out of the elegant salons of the aristocracy and into the realm of everyday middle- and working-class people. This enterprising lady, who was in the habit of offering a cup of tea and a chat to her regular customers when they came in to buy their loaves of bread, persuaded her employers to allow her to create a public tearoom on the premises. Other companies quickly followed suit and soon every high street had its ABC, Express Dairy, Lyons' or Kardomah tearoom. By the 1920s going out to tea was a pastime enjoyed by people from all classes and walks of life. Children who grew up during the Edwardian period have fond memories of tea out with nanny, and most people remember their favourite tearooms with nostalgia and pleasure.

In the grander hotels and restaurants, tea dances became the craze from about 1912 onwards. A demonstration of the tango, which originated in the back streets of Buenos Aires, was given first in Paris and then in London. Initially couples danced between the restaurant tables, but, as the idea caught on, a space was cleared in the middle of the floor. Soon tango-teas and matinees were being held in most hotels and in half a dozen theatres around London. Books were written telling society hostesses how to organize tea dances, restaurants started tango-clubs, and dance teachers, such as Victor Silvester, made their fortunes. One well-known teacher of the time – Miss Gladys Beattie Crozier – wrote in her book *The Tango and How to Dance It*: 'What could be pleasanter on a dull wintry afternoon, at 5 o'clock or so, when calls or shopping are over, than to drop into one of the cheery little Thé Dansant clubs, which have sprung up all over the West End during the last month or two, to take one's place at a tiny table ... set forth with the prettiest of gold and white china, to enjoy a most elaborate and delicious tea served within a moment of one's arrival, while listening to an excellent string band playing delicious haunting airs'.

Sadly, the fashion for tea gradually dwindled, and the tea shops were replaced by fast-food chains with their plastic tables and convenience food.

In the mid-1980s, however, there was a revival of interests: new tea shops opened in unlikely places and quickly became popular; a rash of books about tea including teatime recipes appeared on bookshop shelves; tea dances again became the rage, even in provincial hotels and village halls; and going out for afternoon tea is now very much back in fashion. The National Trust tearooms have carried on regardless through the years of change, but here too there is a difference. The tearooms are expanding, a wider variety of cakes is being baked, and the tea served is now specially packaged for the Trust.

If you have always been a faithful drinker of good old 'British' tea, it is well worth experimenting with some of the speciality brews and blends.

What actually is tea? There are probably more than 10,000 different teas made around the world in more than 35 countries. All of them are made from the leaves and leaf buds of the tea bush, also called the *Camellia sinensis*, a relative of the *Camellia japonica* that we grow in our gardens as a decorative shrub. There are two main varieties that are used to make tea – the *Camellia sinensis sinensis*, a native of China, and the *Camellia sinensis assamica*, a native of Assam in north-east India, and there are about 600 cultivars that have resulted over the centuries from cross-breeding. Each of these grows differently depending on local conditions and each resulting tea will have a different character. Just as all wines vary according to the grape variety used, the growing situation and the manufacturing process used, so all teas vary according to the altitude at which the bushes grow, the seasonal changes, the amount of sunshine, the wind, frost, rainfall and temperature. And as with wines which are blended to give a standard quality and flavour, so teas are blended by the major blending companies to offer the consumer teas that taste the same each time the customer buys them. So your everyday teabag blend can and often does contain teas from Kenya, Malawi, Sri Lanka, India, Indonesia, Argentina and Brazil. The blender selects teas according to quality, taste, price, and the size and appearance of the leaf, and mixes them to give exactly the same taste and quality every time the tea is packed into teabags or cartons.

Just as wines are divided into categories such as white, red, rosé, sparkling and so on, so the many different types of tea are separated according to their manufacture and the main categories are white, green, oolong and black. White teas are made from the tightly furled buds of a particular varietal of the tea bush which pushes out plump buds covered with silvery-white hairs. After plucking, the buds are dried in the sun and packed. They give a pale, champagne-coloured liquor that has a soft, velvety, almost sweet flavour. Green teas are made from the leaves and leaf buds of the tea bush which, after picking, are either steamed or pan-fried to de-enzyme the leaf and then rolled or shaped by hand or machine. Some green teas have needle-like leaves that are dark green, flat and shiny. Gunpowder tea is made by rolling each individual leaf into a tiny ball that looks like a little pellet of lead shot, hence the name. Oolong teas are made by gently shaking or lightly rolling freshly picked and withered leaves and then allowing them to oxidize for a short time before drying. And black teas are made by picking, withering, rolling or chopping the green leaf before allowing it to fully oxidize until it turns to a deep amber brown. Drying in hot ovens removes almost all but 2–3% of the remaining water and the tea is sorted and packed, ready for delivery to the shops and supermarkets.

The most commonly drunk teas in the UK are Darjeeling with its lightly astringent, muscatel quality, Assam with a warm, woody, malty character, Ceylon teas from the island of Sri Lanka with their bright, brisk, golden flavour, English Breakfast style teas that are made from Assam, Ceylon and African teas and offer a depth of flavour that marries well with strongly flavoured foods, smoky Lapsang Souchong from China, and Earl Grey, tea flavoured with essential oil of bergamot. Any white, green, oolong or black tea can be flavoured with fruits, flowers, spices and herbs to make what are called flavoured or scented teas. Although we traditionally add milk to our tea, many teas are better drunk without milk and it is always worth trying the liquor without milk first.

Although tea is drunk and enjoyed throughout the day, the favourite time for many people is at four or five o'clock in the afternoon, when the refreshing cuppa is often accompanied by a sweet or savoury treat. This book offers a wide selection of breads, scones, cakes and biscuits served in National Trust tearooms and restaurants in England, Wales and Northern Ireland, as well as some traditional regional specialities. All are suitable fare for those who, in Samuel Johnson's words, may be 'a hardened and shameless tea-drinker, who has for twenty years diluted his meals with only the infusion of this fascinating plant; whose kettle has scarcely time to cool; who with tea amuses the evening, with tea solaces the midnight, and with tea welcomes the morning.'

Successful Baking

Ingredients

Flour

- Plain flour is generally used when little rise is required; for example, pastries and shortbreads. To convert plain flour to self-raising flour, add baking powder in the quantities recommended on the container for different types of baking.
- Self-raising flour is used for cakes that need a raising agent. In some recipes, however, the amount of raising agent already added to the flour may be too great; a mixture of plain and self-raising flour is therefore used.
- Always store flour in a cool, dry place, preferably in an airtight container. Sift to remove any lumps and also to incorporate extra air before adding to the cake mixture.

Raising agents

- Baking powder is the most commonly used raising agent. It gives off carbon dioxide, which forms bubbles in the mixture. These expand during cooking, making the cake, scone or biscuit rise and helping to produce a light texture. Too much baking powder can cause sogginess and heaviness.
- Bicarbonate of soda is often used in recipes that include sour milk or buttermilk, spices, treacle and honey.
- Sour milk is sometimes necessary to give extra rise to heavy mixtures, such as gingerbreads. It can be made at home by allowing milk to sit in a warm atmosphere until it curdles.
- Buttermilk is a standard ingredient in Welsh and Irish cookery and is available in some supermarkets and from some milk-delivery companies.
- Yeast was once the only raising agent available for home baking, but is now generally used only in bread-making and in some traditional fruit or spice breads or pastries, such as saffron loaves, Chelsea buns and lardy cake. Dried yeast keeps for

several months in an airtight container. Fresh yeast lasts for about a week in the refrigerator and will freeze for up to six months. Fresh yeast is often available from large supermarkets with bakeries, or local bakers. You may have to ask for it as it is not a 'shelf' item, but it is frequently free of charge.

Dried or instant yeast can be substituted for fresh yeast. For 15g (½oz) fresh yeast use 6.25g (¼oz) dried or instant yeast, for 25g (1oz) fresh yeast use 10.5g (½oz) dried or instant yeast and for 50g (2oz) fresh yeast use 21g (¾oz) dried or instant yeast. If using dried yeast, dissolve in a little liquid of the recipe before adding to the other ingredients. If using instant yeast, add to the dry ingredients before mixing in the other ingredients. If using dried or instant yeast, the dough only needs to rise once.

Fats

- Butter and margarine are interchangeable in most recipes, but butter is preferable in shortbreads and rich fruit cakes, such as Christmas cake, that are to be stored for some time and matured.
- Lard is often used in biscuits and gives a shorter texture.
- Oil is excellent in carrot cakes and chocolate cakes, and is ideal for anybody with a cholesterol problem.
- Allow butter, margarine or lard to soften to room temperature for at least an hour before using. Soft or whipped margarines can be used straight from the refrigerator.

Eggs

- Eggs should be at room temperature, as taken straight from the refrigerator they are more likely to curdle.
- Small eggs (sizes 5 and 6) are too small for most recipes. Use large (sizes 1 and 2) or medium (sizes 3 and 4).

Sugar

- Caster sugar is generally used for creamed mixtures as it gives a much lighter texture than other types.
- Granulated sugar is acceptable in rubbed-in mixtures, but can produce a slightly gritty texture. It is worth paying a little extra for caster sugar
- Demerara sugar is very good in tea breads and in mixtures where ingredients are melted together, such as gingerbreads and boiled fruit cakes. It is excellent for sprinkling on the top of loaves and biscuits.
- Soft brown sugar gives a caramel flavour and beats well in creamed mixtures. The darker variety has a stronger flavour.

- Black treacle has a dark colour and strong flavour and is often used in gingerbreads and some fruit cakes.
- Golden syrup gives a soft, moist, sometimes sticky texture which is suitable for gingerbreads and flapjacks.
- Honey adds a very special distinctive flavour but too much will cause the mixture to burn easily.

Preparing tins

Most non-stick cake tins are very reliable if you follow the manufacturers' instructions but, to be on the safe side, it is wise to line and grease them anyway. Grease tins with whatever fat or oil is to be used in the recipe, then line with non-stick greaseproof parchment. Cut a single piece for the bottom of the tin and, when fitting paper to the sides, cut into the corners to make quite sure that it lies neatly against the tin. It may also be necessary to cut and overlap the paper, as the sides of circular tins sometimes slope slightly.

Oven temperatures

Always make sure that the oven has reached the correct temperature before putting in the item to be baked. If you are not sure whether your oven is accurate, buy an oven thermometer and make regular checks. If using a convection oven, reduce all recommended temperatures by 20°C (68°F).

Cakes, scones and biscuits

Always use the right tin for the recipe. Smaller or larger tins will affect the cooking time and hence the texture of the finished cake or biscuits.

Except in fan-assisted ovens, most cakes and biscuits cook best in the middle of the oven. Rich fruit cakes, large cakes and shortbreads should be placed just below the centre, and small, plain cakes, Swiss rolls and scones just above.

Do not disturb the cake during the first three-quarters of the baking time or, better still, not until you think it may be ready. Draughts and knocks can make the cake sink.

When placing biscuits on prepared tins, always allow room for them to spread during baking. It is better to leave too much room than to have all the biscuits merging into one misshapen mass.

Is it ready?

To see if a sponge cake is ready, press lightly with a finger; if it springs back, it is cooked. To test fruitcakes and gingerbreads, stick a skewer into the middle of the cake and withdraw it immediately. If the skewer comes out clean, the cake is done. If not, allow a further 15 minutes and test again. Biscuits are usually ready when they are just turning golden. Scones are firm, well risen and golden when cooked.

If a cake begins to darken too quickly, place a double or triple layer of greaseproof paper over the top and continue cooking as usual.

Pastry

The aim is to make pastry as light as possible, and this depends on how much cold air is trapped in the mixture before baking. The secret is to use cold ingredients, to have cold hands, cold bowls, a cold slab or surface on which to roll (marble is ideal) and to work in a cool room. Work quickly and lightly, using the fingertips when rubbing in, as too much handling makes the pastry tough. When rolling, sprinkle only a little flour on to the work surface and use light, even movements.

Most pastry recipes call for plain flour, but self-raising is sometimes used for suet crust and shortcrust. The more fat is used, the shorter the pastry will be; if the amount of fat is less than half the amount of flour, add 1 teaspoon of baking powder for each 225g (8oz) of flour. Butter, or butter mixed with lard, is best.

Rich pastry needs a hotter oven than others. If the oven is too cool, the fat will run out of the pastry and the pastry will be tough and chewy.

Lining pie dishes and plates

Roll out the pastry to a thickness of about 0.25–0.5cm (⅛–¼in) and a little larger in size than the prepared dish or plate. Lay the pastry carefully on the dish, making sure that no air is trapped underneath. Do not stretch the pastry as it will only shrink back. If it is not big enough, roll out a little more and try again. Ease the pastry into all the rims and corners of the dish, then trim off any surplus. (Trimmings may be useful to make crosses on hot cross buns or a trellis over the top of a tart or pie.)

Raising blind

This is necessary when an uncooked filling is to be put into the pastry case, or to set the pastry before any filling is poured in and cooked. When the prepared tin has been greased and lined with the pastry, prick the base all over with a fork. Cover the base with a piece of greaseproof paper followed by a layer of metal baking beans (available in any good cookware shop) or pasta or pulses (dried haricot beans, dried kidney beans or chickpeas). Bake in a preheated oven for just under the required time, then remove from the oven, lift out the baking beans and the greaseproof paper and bake for 5 minutes more to dry out the base.

Pastry recipes

Flaky pastry
450g (1lb) plain flour, sifted
1 teaspoon salt
350g (12oz) butter, or half butter and half lard, softened
1 teaspoon lemon juice
300ml (10fl oz) cold water

Mix together the flour and salt. Divide the fat into four portions. Rub one portion into the flour with the fingertips. Mix in the lemon juice and cold water to give a soft dough, rather like the consistency of butter. Knead gently on a lightly floured board until smooth. Roll out to a rectangle three times longer than it is wide. Dot the second portion of fat over the top two-thirds of the surface. Fold up the bottom third and fold down the top third and seal the edges by pressing together with a rolling pin. Wrap in cling film or a plastic bag and chill for 15 minutes. Place the dough on the floured board with the folded edges to your right and left, and roll out again to a rectangle. Repeat the dotting, folding and chilling process twice more until all the fat is used. Wrap again and chill for at least 45 minutes before using.

Puff pastry
450g (1lb) plain flour, sifted
1 teaspoon salt
450g (1lb) butter, softened
1 teaspoon lemon juice
75-100ml (3-4fl oz) iced water

Mix together the flour and salt. Add 50g (2oz) of the butter, cut into small pieces, and rub into the flour until the mixture resembles fine breadcrumbs. Add the lemon juice and enough water to give a soft dough, similar to the consistency of butter. Knead lightly until really smooth. In a clean linen cloth, shape the remaining butter into a rectangle. On a lightly floured board, roll out the pastry to a rectangle slightly wider than the rectangle of butter and about twice its length. Place the butter on one half of the pastry and fold the other half over. Press the edges together with a rolling pin. Leave in a cool place for 15 minutes to allow the butter to harden slightly. Roll out the pastry to a long strip three times its original length, but keeping the width the same. The corners should be square, the sides straight and the thickness even. The butter must not break through the dough. Fold the bottom third up and the top third down, press the edges together with a rolling pin, put inside a well-oiled plastic bag and chill for 30 minutes. Place the dough on the floured board with the folded edges to your right and left, and roll out into a long strip as before. Fold again into three and chill for a further 30 minutes. Repeat this process four times more and chill for 30 minutes before using.

This is best made over two days, rolling three times and chilling overnight before completing the rolling the following day.

Rich shortcrust pastry

450g (1lb) plain flour, sifted
a good pinch of salt
350g (12oz) butter, softened
2 egg yolks
4 teaspoons caster sugar
3–4 tablespoons cold water

Mix together the flour and salt. Rub in the butter until the mixture resembles breadcrumbs. Make a well in the middle, add the egg yolks and sugar and mix with a round-bladed knife. Add enough of the water, a little at a time, to give a stiff but pliable dough. Knead lightly until smooth. Wrap in cling film or a plastic bag and chill for at least 15 minutes before using.

Rough puff pastry

450g (1lb) plain flour, sifted
a pinch of salt
350g (12oz) butter, softened
1 teaspoon lemon juice
3–4 tablespoons cold water

Mix together the flour and salt. Cut the butter into small pieces and stir lightly into the flour with a round-bladed knife. Make a well in the middle, add the lemon juice and mix with enough water to give an elastic dough. On a lightly floured board, roll out the dough to a long strip, keeping the sides straight and the corners square. Fold up the bottom third and fold down the top third and turn the dough so that the folded edges are to your right and left. Repeat the rolling and folding process three times more, chilling the pastry for 15 minutes between the third and fourth rolling. Chill for at least 15 minutes before using.

Shortcrust pastry
450g (1lb) plain flour, sifted
a pinch of salt
100g (4oz) butter, softened
100g (4oz) lard, softened
3–4 tablespoons cold water

Mix together the flour and salt. Cut the fats into small pieces and rub into the flour until the mixture resembles fine breadcrumbs. Gradually add enough water, mixing with a fork, to give a stiff, but pliable dough. Knead lightly for a few minutes until smooth. Wrap in cling film or a plastic bag and chill for at least 15 minutes before using.

Bread

Flours

The most commonly used flour for breadmaking is wheat. Strong wheat flour has a high gluten content and gives a better volume of bread, as it absorbs more water and makes a lighter dough. White flour is made from the starchy part of the grain from which the fibre and wheatgerm has been removed. Wholewheat flour is made from 100 per cent of the grain; nothing is added and nothing is taken away. Wheatmeal is made from 81–85 per cent of the grain and some of the fibre and wheatgerm has been removed.

Bread can be made with various other grains. Rye gives a dark dough and is usually mixed half and half with wheat flour; barley gives a cake-like texture and is usually mixed with wheat flour; maize gives a crumbly, crunchy texture. Other ingredients can be added to achieve different results: for example, extra bran, wheatgerm, sesame, poppy or sunflower seeds, cheese, herbs, spices, lemon or orange rind and rye flakes.

Kneading

Kneading is an essential part of breadmaking as it helps to develop the gluten and the rise of the dough. Flour a board and use the palms of the hands, almost to the wrists, to push and turn the dough. As you work you can actually feel the texture changing to a smooth, elastic but not sticky consistency.

Proving

Always cover the dough when setting it to prove; any draughts may affect the process. The yeast in the dough needs warmth to start working; the ideal temperature is between 36 and 44°C (98 and 110°F). Too much heat will kill the yeast; too little will stop it from working. The best place to leave dough to prove is on top of an Aga, a boiler or an active tumble dryer. The time taken for the dough to rise will depend on the warmth, but it usually takes 1–1½ hours. The second rising is quicker, usually between 20 minutes and half an hour.

Baking solutions

Fruit cakes
- If the fruit sinks to the bottom of the cake, it is probably because there was too little beating of fat and sugar, too much liquid or too much raising agent.
- If the cake sinks in the middle, it may be because the oven was not hot enough, or there was too little creaming of fat and sugar, or there was too much raising agent.
- If the cake is dry, it is usually because there was not enough liquid, or it is overcooked.
- If the top of the cake is cracked, the tin was too small and the oven was too hot.

Sandwich and sponge cakes
- If the outside is too dark and the inside is not properly cooked, the oven was too hot and the cake was too near the top.
- If the top of the cake is domed, the oven was too hot or there was not enough beating.
- If the sponge does not rise well, there was either too little raising agent or the oven was too cool.

Scones
- If the scones are tough, there was probably too much kneading.
- If the scones are hard and not spongy, there was too little liquid.
- If the scones are soggy in the middle, the oven was too cool or they were too low in the oven.
- If the scones have not risen, there was too little raising agent.

Yeasted breads and cakes
- If the loaf or cake is smaller than expected, there was either too much or too little raising agent, or the yeast did not activate properly due to incorrect temperature during proving.
- If the texture of the loaf or cake is coarse, the yeast was not properly mixed at the beginning, or there was too much yeast, which caused excessive rising and air in the dough.

Conversions

Weight	Liquid measure	Length	Temperature
15g (½oz)	25ml (1fl oz)	0.5cm (¼in)	110°C, 225°F, gas mark ¼
25g (1oz)	50ml (2fl oz)	1cm (½in)	120°C, 250°F, gas mark ½
50g (2oz)	75ml (3fl oz)	1.5cm (¾in)	140°C, 275°F, gas mark 1
75g (3oz)	100ml (4fl oz)	2.5cm (1in)	150°C, 300°F, gas mark 2
100g (4oz)	150ml (5fl oz or ¼ pint)	5cm (2in)	160°C, 325°F, gas mark 3
150g (5oz)	300ml (10fl oz or ½ pint)	7.5cm (3in)	180°C, 350°F, gas mark 4
175g (6oz)	350ml (12fl oz)	10cm (4in)	190°C, 375°F, gas mark 5
200g (7oz)	400ml (15fl oz)	12.5cm (5in)	200°C, 400°F, gas mark 6
225g (8oz)	600ml (20fl oz or 1 pint)	15cm (6in)	220°C, 425°F, gas mark 7
250g (9oz)		17.5cm (7in)	230°C, 450°F, gas mark 8
275g (10oz)		20cm (8in)	240°C, 475°F, gas mark 9
300g (11oz)		22.5cm (9in)	
350g (12oz)		25cm (10in)	
375g (13oz)		27.5cm (11in)	
400g (14oz)		30cm (12in)	
425g (15oz)			
450g (1lb)			
675g (1½lb)			
900g (2lb)			

These approximate conversions are used throughout this book.

Use a standard tea cup for measuring.

American Equivalents

Dry measures

1 US cup	50g (2oz)	breadcrumbs; cake crumbs
1 US cup	75g (3oz)	porridge or rolled oats
1 US cup	90g (3½oz)	ground almonds; shredded coconut
1 US cup	100g (4oz)	roughly chopped walnuts and other nuts; icing sugar; cocoa; drinking chocolate; flaked almonds; grated Cheddar cheese
1 US cup	150g (5oz)	white flour; currants; rice flour; muesli; cornflour; chopped dates
1 US cup	175g (6oz)	wholemeal flour; oatmeal; raisins; sultanas; dried apricots; mixed candied peel
1 US cup	200g (7oz)	caster sugar; soft brown sugar; demerara sugar; rice; glacé cherries; semolina; chopped figs or plums
1 US cup	225g (8oz)	granulated sugar; curd cheese; cream cheese
1 US cup	300g (11oz)	mincemeat; marmalade; jam
1 US cup	350g (12oz)	golden syrup; black treacle

Liquid measures

⅛ US cup	25g (1fl oz)
¼ US cup	50g (2fl oz)
½ US cup	100g (4fl oz)
1 US cup	220g (8fl oz)
1¼ US cups	300g (10fl oz)
1¾ US cups	400g (15fl oz)
2 US cups	475g (16fl oz)
2½ US cups	600g (20fl oz)

Measures for fats

¼ stick	25g
1 stick (½ US cup)	100g

Breads

When tea was first served in England in the 17th century and for the 150 years or so of domestic tea drinking, the only food served with tea was elegantly thin slices of bread and butter. As afternoon tea became more and more important during the 19th century, fresh breads played an important part on the tea table in the form of neat, crustless sandwiches filled with chicken, egg mayonnaise, baked ham, thinly sliced cucumber and smoked salmon. Today, ubiquitous plastic packs of dull white and brown breads leave us yearning for the flavour and texture of days gone by.

Organic Wholewheat Bread

This lovely nutty-flavoured bread comes from Branscombe Bakery, the last traditional bakery to be used in Devon. Until 1987 it was run by brothers Gerald and Stuart Collier who baked bread, buns, cakes, tarts and scones every day of the year. The oven was lit at four o'clock every morning and then, three hours later when it had reached the required temperature, the ashes were raked out, the oven cleaned and then the first batch of 130 loaves arranged inside.

25g (1oz) fresh yeast (to substitute dried yeast, see page 11)
½ teaspoon light or dark soft brown sugar
600–750ml (1–1¼ pints) warm water (it should be almost hand-hot, and the
    amount needed varies according to the flour used)
900g (2lb) organic wholemeal flour, sifted and warmed slightly in the oven
1 tablespoon sea salt
1 tablespoon corn or sunflower oil
1 tablespoon clear honey

Makes 2 x 900g (2lb) loaves

Cream together the yeast and sugar and blend with 50–75ml (2–3fl oz) of the warm water. Leave in a warm, draught-free place for 10–20 minutes until frothy – there should be at least 1.5cm (¾in) of froth on the top. Mix together the flour and salt and make a well in the middle. Pour in the oil, honey, yeast mixture and enough of the remaining water to give a soft, elastic dough. Knead with the hands for about 10 minutes. Shape the dough into a ball and place in a lightly greased bowl. Dust the top with a little flour, cover with a clean damp cloth and leave in a warm, draught-free place until almost doubled in size (this can take anything from 50 minutes to 2 hours). Grease two 900g (2lb) loaf tins. Turn the dough out on to a lightly floured board and knead vigorously for 8–10 minutes. Divide the dough into two equal portions and shape to fit the tins. Place in the tins, sprinkle the tops with a little more flour and cover with a clean damp cloth. Leave in a warm place for a further 30–40 minutes until the dough reaches the top of the tins. Meanwhile heat the oven to 220°C, 425°F, gas mark 7. When the dough has risen, bake the loaves for 30 minutes. Remove from the oven and remove from the tins. Place the loaves in the oven for a further 10–15 minutes until they sound hollow when tapped. Remove from the oven and cool on a wire rack.

Boxty Bread

Boxty bread is traditional festive Irish bread, flat and round and marked into four portions before baking to allow for easy division once cooked. With potatoes its essentially Irish ingredient, it was once an indulgence for Shrove Tuesday, All Saints' Day or Hallowe'en.

225g (8oz) raw potatoes
225g (8oz) mashed potatoes
225g (8oz) plain flour, sifted
50g (2oz) butter, melted
Salt and freshly ground black pepper

Makes 2 small round flat loaves

Preheat the oven to 190°C, 375°F, gas mark 5. Grease a baking tray. Wash and peel the raw potatoes. Grate into a clean cloth and wring well over a bowl to squeeze out the juice. Place the grated potatoes in a bowl with the mashed potatoes and mix well together. Leave the starchy liquid in the bowl until the starch has settled, then pour off the liquid and add the starch to the potatoes. Add the flour, melted butter and seasoning and mix to a soft dough. Knead well. Divide into two portions and, on a floured board, roll into flat rounds. Place on the baking tray and divide the top of each loaf into four with a sharp knife. Bake for 40 minutes until firm and golden. Remove from the oven and serve hot with plenty of butter.

Bateman's Soda Bread

A soft, light bread, this recipe is from Rudyard Kipling's Jacobean house in East Sussex.

225g (8oz) plain wholemeal flour, sifted

2 teaspoons baking powder

½ teaspoon salt

1 teaspoon demerara sugar

25g (1oz) butter, softened

150ml (5fl oz) milk

Cracked wheat, oatmeal or oats

Makes 1 x 15cm (6in) round loaf

Preheat the oven to 200°C, 400°F, gas mark 6. Grease a baking tray. Mix together the flour, baking powder, salt and sugar and rub in the butter. Add the milk and mix to a soft dough. Shape into a round and place on the prepared tray. Brush the top with a little milk and sprinkle with cracked wheat, oatmeal or oats. Bake for 20–30 minutes until well risen and browned. Remove from the oven and serve warm with butter.

Herb Bread

225g (8oz) self-raising white or wholemeal flour (or a mixture of half and half), sifted

1 teaspoon dry English mustard powder

2 tablespoons fresh chopped herbs (chives, thyme, basil, sage, parsley)

100g (4oz) mature Cheddar cheese, grated

25g (1oz) butter

1 egg, beaten

150ml (5fl oz) water

Makes 1 x 450g (1lb) loaf

Preheat the oven to 190°C, 375°F, gas mark 5. Grease a 450g (1lb) loaf tin. Mix together the flour, mustard, herbs and cheese. Melt the butter, add to the mixture with the egg and water and mix to a soft, wet, cake-like dough. Turn into the prepared tin and bake for 45 minutes until well risen and golden brown. Remove from the oven and cool on a wire rack. Serve warm or cold with butter.

Right: Herb Bread
Next page: Bara Brith

Buttermilk Oaten Bread

Fine oatmeal gives a wonderful gritty texture to this favourite Irish bread. Buttermilk was once a staple ingredient in breads and cakes, and gave a slightly sour taste and good keeping qualities. Serve this as a satisfying part of 'high tea', warm with cheese or toasted with melting butter and thick fruity jams.

200g (7oz) fine oatmeal
300ml (10fl oz) buttermilk
125ml (4fl oz) milk
250g (9oz) plain flour, sifted
1 teaspoon baking powder
¼ teaspoon salt

Makes 2 small loaves

Soak the oatmeal in the buttermilk and milk overnight. The following day preheat the oven to 180°C, 350°F, gas mark 4. Grease a baking tray. Mix together the flour, baking powder and salt. Add the oatmeal and milk mixture and mix well to give a soft dough. Knead until smooth. Divide into two portions and, on a floured board, roll each portion out to a thickness of about 2.5cm (1in) and about 10cm (4in) in diameter. Place both loaves on the prepared tray and bake for 35–40 minutes until they are golden and sound hollow when tapped. Remove from the oven and serve hot with butter.

This is an easy and quick bread to make; it has a soft, moist texture and a lovely, nutty flavour.

Left: Buttermilk Oaten Bread
Previous page: Barm Brack

Bara Brith

Bara Brith is the traditional tea loaf of Wales, easy to prepare and delicious sliced and spread with butter. This recipe comes from Erddig, a great Georgian house visited on 16th August 1921 by Queen Mary who took afternoon tea in the dining room after touring the ground floor rooms and visiting the servants' hall. Perhaps she ate Bara Brith in true Welsh style that day!

350g (12oz) mixed dried fruit
350ml (12fl oz) red wine
100g (4oz) butter
100g (4oz) light soft brown sugar
50ml (2fl oz) milk
1 tablespoon black treacle
225g (8oz) self-raising flour, sifted
1 teaspoon mixed spice
2 eggs, beaten

Makes 1 x 900g (2lb) loaf

Soak the fruit in the red wine overnight. The next day preheat the oven to 180°C, 350°F, gas mark 4. Grease and line a 900g (2lb) loaf tin. Add the butter, sugar, milk and treacle to the fruit, bring to the boil and simmer for 5 minutes. Remove from the heat and leave to cool. Add the flour, mixed spice and beaten eggs and beat well with a wooden spoon. Turn into the prepared tin and bake just below the middle of the oven for 1–1¼ hours until a skewer comes out clean. Remove from the oven and leave to cool in the tin for 15 minutes before turning out on to a wire rack to cool completely. Serve sliced with butter.

   Each region has its own version of this traditional Welsh tea bread. This one may be made with cold tea instead of red wine.

Barm Brack

Another good example of the use of succulent dried fruits and candied peel to make a plain cake more interesting. Barm means 'leaven' or 'yeast' and Brack means speckled and refers to the fruit scattered through the dough. It was often made in flattened rounds and is served sliced, sometimes toasted and spread with plenty of butter. At Hallowe'en, a small coin, pea, ring or stick was concealed in the dough to predict the fortune of the person who found it – the coin meant riches, the pea meant no marriage, the ring foretold a wedding and the stick indicated an unhappy marriage!

100g (4oz) currants
100g (4oz) sultanas
100g (4oz) raisins
50g (2oz) mixed candied peel
50g (2oz) glacé cherries, quartered
200g (7oz) light soft brown sugar
300ml (10fl oz) cold black tea
Grated rind of 1 lemon
2 eggs, beaten
250g (9oz) self-raising flour, sifted
1 teaspoon mixed spice
Pinch of salt

Makes 1 x 900g (2lb) loaf

Put the dried fruit and glace cherries into a bowl with the sugar, tea and lemon rind and leave to soak for at least 3 hours, preferably longer. Preheat the oven to 180°C, 350°F, gas mark 4. Grease and line a 900g (2lb) loaf tin. Add the eggs, flour, mixed spice and salt to the fruit mixture and mix thoroughly. Turn into the prepared tin and bake for 1½–1¾ hours until a skewer comes out clean. Remove from the oven and turn out on to a wire rack to cool. Serve sliced with butter.

Raisin and Bran Bread

A low-fat tea bread, this is made to a recipe from Standen, the Sussex Arts and Crafts home designed by Philip Webb, one of William Morris' closest friends. This was almost the last house he ever built but some of the same features he used in his original commission, Morris' Red House, are echoed in its architecture. At the time the house was built in the 1890s, interior design was heavily influenced by oriental style and on show in the drawing room is a delicate Japanese tea service. Japanese Buddhist priests often spent time travelling in China to study their religion and, having discovered tea, took it back home and introduced it to the Japanese monasteries. Tea drinking became popular among the Japanese people in the 11th and 12th centuries AD and the method of whisking powdered matcha *green tea into bowls of hot water evolved into a ritualized ceremony known as* Cha-no-yu, *'the way of tea'.*

75g (3oz) bran cereal (All Bran or similar)
75g (3oz) sugar
175g (6oz) raisins
300ml (10fl oz) milk
175g (6oz) wholemeal self-raising flour, sifted
50–75ml (2–3fl oz) milk and water mixed in equal measures

Makes 1 x 900g (2lb) loaf

Put the bran cereal, sugar, raisins and milk into a bowl and leave overnight (or for at least 6 hours), stirring occasionally. Preheat the oven to 160°C, 325°F, gas mark 3. Grease and line a 900g (2lb) loaf tin. Add the flour to the soaked ingredients and mix with enough of the milk and water to give a runny consistency. Pour into the prepared tin and bake for 1 hour. Remove from the oven and leave to cool in the tin.

The bran gives this bread a pleasant, rather coarse texture. It contains very little fat and sugar and is therefore ideal for anybody who is concerned about cholesterol or calories.

Derbyshire Spiced Easter Fruit Bread

Many of our traditional fruited celebration cakes originated as plain bread mixtures which were enriched for special occasions with dried fruit, cream, spices and butter – all of which were too expensive to use every day. This Easter bread is a perfect example of readily available ingredients such as flour, lard and milk combined with more costly dates, sultanas, sugar and cinnamon.

225g (8oz) self-raising flour, sifted
1 teaspoon mixed spice
½ teaspoon ground cinnamon
75g (3oz) lard, softened
75g (3oz) sugar
50g (2oz) sultanas
50g (2oz) dates, chopped
1 egg, beaten
6 tablespoons milk

Makes 1 x 900g (2lb) loaf

Preheat the oven to 190°C, 375°F, gas mark 5. Grease and line a 900g (2lb) loaf tin. Mix together the flour and spices. Chop the lard into very small pieces and cut roughly into the flour with a knife. Add the sugar, sultanas, dates, egg and milk and mix to a soft consistency. Turn into the prepared tin and bake for 40–45 minutes until a skewer comes out clean. Remove from the oven and turn out on to a wire rack to cool. Serve sliced with butter.

Date and Walnut Loaf

This Cornish recipe from Cotehele in Cornwall is typical in its use of spices, brown sugar and exotic fruit. From the 17th century, ships from the Orient imported such luxuries through the Cornish ports and many cake recipes from the region include ginger, cinnamon, nutmeg, dried dates and raisins. Cotehele would certainly have known about such ingredients, sitting as it does close to the River Tamar which for centuries was the only effective route to the outside world. The immense oven in the north wall of the kitchen almost certainly baked a number of these loaves over the centuries.

225g (8oz) self-raising flour, sifted
50g (2oz) whole walnuts
1 teaspoon mixed spice
75g (3oz) butter, softened
100g (4oz) light or dark soft brown sugar
225g (8oz) whole dates
150ml (5fl oz) water
2 eggs, beaten
2 tablespoons sesame seeds

Makes 1 x 900g (2lb) loaf

Preheat the oven to 180°C, 350°F, gas mark 4. Grease and line a 900g (2lb) loaf tin. Mix together the flour, walnuts and mixed spice. Place the butter, sugar, dates and water in a pan and bring gently to the boil. Remove from the heat and cool for a few minutes. Add to the flour, spice and nuts with the beaten eggs and beat well. Turn into the prepared tin, hollow the middle a little and sprinkle the top with the sesame seeds. Bake for 1–1¼ hours until a skewer comes out clean. Remove from the oven and turn out on to a wire rack to cool. Serve sliced with butter.

Irish Potato Cakes

Irish recipes make inventive use of potatoes and working people relied heavily on recipes that mixed them with milk, buttermilk, cream and eggs to make breads and cakes and these traditional savouries. Other traditional potato specialities include 'dippity', a mixture of raw grated potatoes, flour, milk, eggs and salt cooked in little round cakes, 'champ', made with mashed potatoes, spring onions, milk and butter, and 'boxty', a mixture of potatoes cooked as pancakes, dumplings or bread.

100g (4oz) cold mashed potatoes
100g (4oz) plain white flour, sifted
50g (2oz) lard or dripping
Pinch of salt
A little milk

Makes 6 cakes

Preheat the oven to 200°C, 400°F, gas mark 6. Grease a baking tray. Mix together the potatoes and flour and rub in the fat. Add the salt and enough milk to give a soft, pliable dough. Roll out on a floured board to a thickness of 1cm (½in) and cut into rounds using a 6cm (2½in) cutter. Place on the prepared tray and bake for 15–20 minutes until golden. Remove from the oven and serve piping hot, spread with butter.

These traditional savoury cakes are excellent served for breakfast, tea or supper.

Cheese and Celery Whirls

This recipe comes from Longshaw Estate in South Yorkshire where homemade breads would have taken an important place on the 'high tea' table. Workers in the nearby quarries and mills would have been ravenous when they returned home at 5.30pm and so tucked in to meat pies, thick slices of ham, chunks of cheese and home baked breads and cakes – all washed down with several cups of strong black tea with milk and sugar. Whereas 'afternoon tea' was an upper class, elegant, social occasion, 'high tea' was designed to satisfy the hunger that followed an eight- or ten-hour shift in one of the local mills or factories.

350g (12oz) self-raising flour, sifted
1 teaspoon salt
½ teaspoon dry English mustard powder
50g (2oz) butter, softened
100g (4oz) mature Cheddar cheese, grated
1 garlic clove (or more to taste), crushed
1 egg, beaten
150ml (5fl oz) milk
3–4 sticks of celery, washed and roughly chopped

Makes approximately 10–12 whirls

Preheat the oven to 220°C, 425°F, gas mark 7. Mix together the flour, salt and mustard powder. Rub in the butter until the mixture resembles breadcrumbs. Add most of the grated cheese (reserving a little for sprinkling on top), garlic, beaten egg and milk and mix well so that all the ingredients are evenly distributed. On a floured board, knead lightly and then roll out to a rectangle approximately 22.5 x 30cm (9 x 12in). Scatter the celery over the surface. Roll up like a Swiss roll, starting with the narrow edge. Cut slices approximately 1.5cm (½in) thick, lay them flat on the prepared baking trays and sprinkle a little of the remaining cheese over the surface of each. Bake for 15–20 minutes until golden and well risen. Remove from the oven and serve warm.

These pretty whirls make an excellent accompaniment to a dinner party starter or they are suitable served as a teatime savoury. They are beautifully light and extremely tasty.

Right: Cheese and Celery Whirls

Suffolk Fourses

*During the harvest each year in England's eastern counties, the farmers' wives worked hard
to produce four or five meals a day to feed the hungry local and itinerant workers. Flasks of
tea and bottles of cold homemade lemonade were carried out in bags and baskets by the
women and children for the midday and mid-afternoon meals. Everyone stopped work,
found somewhere to rest in the shade of a nearby haystack and devoured the freshly baked
breads, rolls and cakes.*

25g (1oz) fresh yeast (to substitute dried yeast, see page 11)
1 teaspoon caster sugar
300ml (10fl oz) milk
900g (2lb) plain flour, sifted
½ teaspoon salt
50g (2oz) lard, softened
100g (4oz) caster, granulated or demerara sugar
100g (4oz) currants or raisins
Pinch of mixed spice
175g (6oz) butter
3 eggs, well beaten
Caster or demerara sugar for dredging

Makes approximately 16 cakes

Cream the yeast with the teaspoon of caster sugar. Warm the milk and add to the yeast. Mix together
the flour and salt and rub in the fat. Add the sugar, currants or raisins and spice and mix well. Melt
the butter and stir into the beaten eggs. Add to the milk and yeast mixture and pour into the flour.
Mix with a round-bladed knife to a light dough. Cover the bowl with a clean damp cloth and leave
in a warm place for about 2 hours until the dough has doubled in size. Meanwhile grease two baking
trays. When the dough has risen knead on a lightly floured board, then roll out to a thickness of
approximately 1.5cm (⅝in) and cut into rounds 10cm (4in) in diameter. Place on the prepared trays
and leave to rise in a warm place for 30 minutes. Meanwhile heat the oven to 200°C, 400°F, gas mark
6. When the fourses have risen, mark the tops into four sections and dredge with caster or demerara
sugar. Bake for 15–20 minutes until firm and golden. Remove from the oven and eat either warm or
cold, split and buttered.

Left: Suffolk Fourses

Sesame Rolls

From Trerice in Cornwall, these little rolls enjoy the sweet nuttiness of sesame and are delicious at teatime filled with smoked salmon or honey roast ham. The glory of Trerice is the south-facing drawing room – a perfect room in which to take tea. Displayed here are some fine examples of Chinese porcelain tea bowls and little pots that were imported on the same ships that brought the chests of tea from the Orient. European potters were amazed at the fine, translucent quality of the Chinese wares when they first came across them in the middle of the 17th century and spent the following fifty years or so attempting to manufacture something equally beautiful.

15g (½oz) fresh yeast (to substitute dried yeast, see page 11)

2 teaspoons caster sugar

400ml (15fl oz) water, warmed

675g (1½lb) strong plain white flour, sifted

1½ teaspoons full-cream milk powder (Coffeemate or similar)

½ teaspoon salt

25g (1oz) butter, softened

1 egg, beaten, mixed with a little water

2–3 tablespoons sesame seeds

Makes approximately 14 rolls

Mix together the yeast, sugar and 75ml (3fl oz) of the water. Leave in a warm place for about 20–30 minutes until frothy. Mix together the flour, milk powder and salt and rub in the fat. Add the yeast mixture and the remaining water and mix to a pliable dough. Knead until smooth and elastic, then place in a bowl, cover with a damp cloth and leave in a warm place for 1–1½ hours until doubled in size. Grease two baking trays. When the dough is well risen, divide into 65g (2½oz) pieces, form these into bun shapes and place on the prepared trays. Brush the tops with egg wash and sprinkle liberally with sesame seeds. Leave in a warm place for about 30 minutes until well risen. Meanwhile heat the oven to 200°C, 400°F, gas mark 6. When the rolls are well risen, bake for 20–25 minutes until golden brown and firm. Remove from the oven and lift on to a wire rack to cool. Serve warm or cold.

If liked stir a tablespoon of sesame seeds into the dough with the yeast mixture. Sprinkle as above with more seeds before baking.

Sweet Wholemeal Bannock

*Irish teatimes demanded all the same treats as were enjoyed throughout Britain from about
1840 when Anna Maria, the 7th Duchess of Bedford, is said to have named the mid-afternoon
indulgence of a pot of tea and a little something to eat. During the first 200 years of tea
drinking in England, the only food offered with tea had been thin slices of bread and butter,
but once afternoon tea and high tea became popular during the 19th century, the teatime
menu gradually became more elaborate with sandwiches, scones, muffins, dainty pastries,
biscuits and cakes.*

350g (12oz) plain wholemeal flour, sifted
100g (4oz) plain white flour, sifted
1 teaspoon bicarbonate of soda
50g (2oz) butter, softened
2 dessertspoons caster sugar
200ml (7fl oz) buttermilk

Makes 1 x 900g (2lb) loaf or 1 x 20cm (8in) round bannock

Preheat the oven to 180°C, 350°F, gas mark 4. Grease and line a 900g (2lb) loaf tin or a 20cm (8in)
round tin. Mix together the flours and bicarbonate of soda and rub in the butter. Add the sugar and
mix with the buttermilk to give a soft, pliable dough. Knead lightly, then shape to fit the tin. Place
in the tin and bake for 35–45 minutes until well risen and golden. Remove from the oven and turn
out on to a wire rack to cool. Serve warm, sliced and spread with butter.

Kentish Huffkins

Huffkins were traditionally baked in the kitchens of Kentish farms and carried out to the hop fields to feed the bands of seasonal workers from the East End of London who arrived each year for their annual working holiday. The indented middle of each huffkin was usually filled with stewed cherries or apples from the nearby orchards.

450g (1lb) plain flour, sifted
½ teaspoon salt
25g (1oz) lard, softened
25g (1oz) fresh yeast (to substitute dried yeast, see page 11)
1 teaspoon caster sugar
350ml (12fl oz) milk, or a mixture of milk and water, warmed

Makes 12 huffkins

Grease two baking trays. Sift together the flour and salt and rub in the lard. Cream the yeast with the sugar and add to the warmed milk (or milk and water). Add to the flour and mix to a light, soft dough. Leave in a warm place for about 1 hour until doubled in size. On a floured board, knead the dough lightly, then divide into twelve flat oval cakes about 1cm (½in) thick. Place on the prepared trays and leave in a warm place for about 30 minutes until well risen. Meanwhile heat the oven to 200°C, 400°F, gas mark 6. When the huffkins are well risen, make a hole with your thumb in the middle of each and bake for 10–20 minutes until lightly browned and firm. Remove from the oven and cover immediately with a clean, dry cloth until cold; this helps to keep the rolls soft.

Honey Tea Bread

The drawing room at Kingston Lacy in Devon, whose recipe this is, is laid out as it was in 1900 and includes a silver tea service on a tray with a kettle standing over its little burner. Since tea was, until the late 19th century, a very expensive commodity, the lady of the house never allowed her servants to brew the tea but took charge herself of the leaf, the kettle and the teapot. The locked tea caddy of mother-of-pearl, tortoise shell, ivory, crystal or precious woods was kept in the drawing room away from the potential pilfering of the housemaids.

FOR THE LOAF
225g (8oz) mixed dried fruit
150ml (5fl oz) cold tea
100g (4oz) clear honey
225g (8oz) self-raising flour, sifted
1 egg, well beaten
100g (4oz) butter, melted

FOR THE TOPPING
1 tablespoon honey, warmed
25g (1oz) finely chopped nuts (walnuts, hazelnuts or almonds)
25g (1oz) demerara sugar

Makes 1 x 900g (2lb) loaf

Place the dried fruit, tea and honey in a bowl and leave to soak overnight or for at least 6 hours. Preheat the oven to 150°C, 300°F, gas mark 2. Grease and line a 900g (2lb) loaf tin. Mix the flour into the fruit mixture. Add the beaten egg and beat hard. Finally, beat in the melted butter. Turn into the prepared tin and bake for 50 minutes. Remove from the oven and prepare the topping. Brush with the warmed honey, mix together the nuts and sugar and sprinkle over the top. Return to the oven and bake for a further 15–20 minutes until a skewer comes out clean. Remove from the oven and leave to cool in the tin. When cool, carefully remove from the tin and serve sliced with butter.

Saffron Cake

In the 14th century, vast fields of blue crocuses were grown in Essex to produce home-grown saffron. But when saffron began to feature among the exotic goods being imported to England through ports along the Cornish coast, the trade moved to the West Country. Cornwall is rich in recipes for saffron buns, cakes and fruit loaves that were particularly popular during Lent, at Easter and as fairings at annual fairs. This is another Cotehele recipe and, as with the spices and dried fruits used in the Date and Walnut Loaf (see page 30), the family who lived there would have used saffron as an ingredient for special occasions.

15g (½oz) fresh yeast (to substitute dried yeast, see page 11)
32g (1¼oz) caster sugar
175ml (6fl oz) water, warmed
7g (¼oz) low-fat, freeze-dried milk powder
250g (9oz) strong plain white flour, sifted
7g (¼oz) saffron, ground and soaked for several hours
    in 2 teaspoons warm water
Generous pinch of salt
65g (2½ oz) butter, softened
65–75g (2½–3oz) currants
40–50g (1½–2oz) mixed candied peel

Makes 1 x 900g (2lb) loaf

Cream together the yeast and caster sugar and mix with the warm water, milk powder and 25g (1oz) of the flour. Whisk, then leave in a warm place for 30 minutes until frothy and doubled in size. Strain the saffron, add with all the other ingredients to the yeast mixture and beat well to a fairly elastic dough. Leave in a warm place for a further 40–50 minutes until doubled in size. Grease a 900g (2lb) loaf tin. Turn the mixture into the tin and stand in a warm place for 30 minutes to rise almost to the top of the tin. Meanwhile heat the oven to 180°C, 350°F, gas mark 4. When the dough has risen, bake for 50 minutes to 1 hour until a skewer comes out clean. Remove from the oven and turn out on to a wire rack to cool. This saffron loaf is not very sweet and, spread with butter and honey or preserves, it makes an ideal tea bread.

Ripon Christmas Bread

Another traditional enriched bread dough, this festive loaf from Yorkshire, includes allspice in the ingredients. Also called Jamaican Pepper or newspice, it is the dried unripe fruit of Pimenta dioica plant. Its aroma and taste combines the complex characters of cinnamon and cloves and adds a slightly hotter, peppery quality.

FOR THE BASIC BREAD DOUGH
900g (2lb) plain flour, sifted
2 teaspoons salt
25g (1oz) fresh yeast (to substitute dried yeast, see page 11)
1 teaspoon caster sugar
100g (4oz) butter, softened
600ml (1 pint) milk, warmed

FOR THE ADDITIONAL FLAVOURING
175g (6oz) lard, softened and cut into small pieces
100g (4oz) raisins
50g (2oz) mixed candied peel
100g (4oz) granulated or caster sugar
225g (8oz) currants
½ teaspoon allspice

Makes 2 x 900g (2lb) loaves

First make the basic bread dough. Mix together the flour and salt. Cream the yeast with the sugar. Rub the fat into the flour, add the yeast and warm milk and mix to a light dough. Knead well with floured hands until smooth. Place the dough in a bowl and stand in a warm place for 1½–2 hours until doubled in size. Grease two 900g (2lb) loaf tins. Mix together all the additional ingredients and work into the dough until all are evenly distributed. Divide the mixture between the tins and leave in a warm place until the dough almost reaches the top of the tins. Meanwhile heat the oven to 160°C, 325°F, gas mark 3. When the loaves are well risen, bake for approximately 2 hours until golden and firm. Remove from the oven and turn out on to a wire rack to cool. Serve either warm or cold and spread with butter.

In most areas of Britain in the past, large batches of fruit loaves were baked at Christmas ready to feed the family and any visitors who called at the house between Christmas and New Year.

Orange Tea Bread

This recipe is from Moseley Old Hall in Staffordshire, an Elizabethan house where Charles II successfully hid from Parliamentarian soldiers after the Royalist defeat at the Battle of Worcester in 1651. From the tea drinker's point of view, it is just as well that he managed to survive that episode and his exile in northern Europe, for after his return to England, he married Catherine of Braganza who introduced tea to the English court. Born in Portugal, Catherine was an avid tea drinker long before the English had even heard of the drink, and when she arrived in England in 1662 for her wedding she brought a chest of tea with her, served it to her aristocratic friends and set a new fashion.

75g (3oz) butter, softened
225g (8oz) self-raising flour (white or wholemeal), sifted
75g (3oz) caster sugar
50g (2oz) walnuts, roughly chopped
1 large egg, beaten
2 oranges (the grated rind of both, the juice from one
    and the other left whole)
2 tablespoons caster sugar for sprinkling

Makes 1 x 900g (2lb) loaf

Preheat the oven to 180°C, 350°F, gas mark 4. Grease and line a 900g (2lb) loaf tin. Rub the butter into the flour until the mixture resembles fine breadcrumbs. Stir in the sugar and walnuts. Add the egg, orange rind and juice and beat well. Turn into the prepared tin. Holding the remaining orange over the tin so as to catch any juice, remove the skin and pith and divide into segments. Arrange over the top of the cake and sprinkle with the caster sugar. Bake for 1¼–1½ hours until a skewer comes out clean. Remove from the oven and leave to cool in the tin.

Blackberry Tea Bread

*Made with freshly harvested hedgerow berries, this tea loaf from Trelissick in Cornwall
makes a delicious change from more traditional fruited breads. The garden here was created
by Ronald Copeland who was chairman, and later managing director, of the Spode china
factory. Many of the flowers that flourish in the mild Cornish air were the inspiration for the
floral designs produced at the works.*

350g (12oz) plain flour, sifted
1 teaspoon mixed spice
175g (6oz) butter, softened
175g (6oz) caster sugar
225g (8oz) fresh or frozen blackberries
   (if frozen, use straight from the freezer)
Grated rind and juice of 1 lemon
1 tablespoon black treacle
2 eggs, beaten
½ teaspoon bicarbonate of soda
2 tablespoons milk

Makes 1 x 900g (2lb) loaf

Preheat the oven to 180°C, 350°F, gas mark 4. Grease and line a 900g (2lb) loaf tin. Mix together the
flour and mixed spice and rub in the butter until the mixture bears a resemblance to fine
breadcrumbs. Add the sugar, blackberries, lemon rind and juice, treacle and eggs and mix well.
Dissolve the bicarbonate of soda in the milk, add to the mixture and beat well. Pour into the prepared
tin, level and bake for 45 minutes. Reduce the oven temperature to 150°C, 300°F, gas mark 2 and
cook for a further 30–45 minutes until a skewer comes out clean. Remove from the oven and leave
in the tin for about 15 minutes before turning out on to a wire rack to cool.

   This unusual loaf is an ideal and novel way of using the blackberries that flourish in our
hedgerows every summer.

Fruited Buns, Scones, Muffins and Splits

Many of our traditional fruited buns such as tea cakes, Chelsea Buns and Bath Buns started life centuries ago as plainer breads that were enriched for festive occasions such as Easter, Christmas, New Year and saints days by adding expensive spices, dried fruits, butter and sugar to basic doughs. Today, the wonderful variety of textures and flavours offered by all these easy recipes are perfect with an afternoon cup of tea.

Hot Cross Buns

Although this Easter recipe is from Trerice in Cornwall, the spiced buns are of course traditional throughout Britain. Among the spices used is nutmeg which, during Elizabethan times, was believed to ward off plague and was therefore so valuable that a few nutmeg could be sold for enough money to set you up financially for the rest of your life.

FOR THE BUNS
25g (1oz) fresh yeast (to substitute dried yeast, see page 11)
50g (2oz) caster sugar
400ml (15fl oz) milk and water, mixed and warmed
50g (2oz) butter, softened
675g (1½lb) strong plain white flour, sifted
Pinch of salt
225g (8oz) mixed dried fruit
100g (4oz) mixed candied peel
2 teaspoons mixed spice
2 teaspoons grated nutmeg

FOR THE TOPPING
1 tablespoon caster sugar
1 tablespoon cold water
Thick paste made with 75g (3oz) plain flour and
    3 tablespoons water (or trimmings from short pastry)

Makes 18 buns

Cream the yeast with the sugar and add 150ml (5fl oz) of the milk and water mixture. Stir well, then leave in a warm place for 20–30 minutes until frothy. Grease three baking trays. Rub the butter into the flour and add the salt, mixed dried fruit, peel, mixed spice and nutmeg. When the yeast mixture is frothy, add to the dry ingredients with the remaining milk and water. Mix to a stiff dough and knead on a floured board until smooth. Form the dough into 75g (3oz) balls and place on the prepared trays. Leave in a warm place for about 30 minutes until almost doubled in size. Meanwhile preheat the oven to 220°C, 425°F, gas mark 7. Mix together the caster sugar and water for the topping. Make the stiff paste with the flour and water and roll out on a floured board. Cut narrow strips ready to make the crosses for the tops of the buns. When the buns have risen, carefully brush the tops with sugar and water and place a cross on each. Bake for 15 minutes until nicely browned. Remove from the oven and lift on to a wire rack to cool. Serve warm with butter.

Sue's Amazing Rock Cakes

A rough sort of scone, this recipe comes from Claremont Landscape Gardens in Surrey, one of England's finest gardens to be designed to blend with its surrounding natural landscape. Laid out around a lake, it has open glades and dense woodland, shaded serpentine pathways, a turf amphitheatre and a pavilion which may well have been the setting for 18th-century tea parties. Follies, grottos and temples were strategically placed in the park or gardens surrounding grand houses to provide a peaceful venue where tea was served after the main meal of the day.

225g (8oz) plain wholewheat flour, sifted

100g (4oz) plain white flour, sifted

4 teaspoons baking powder

1 teaspoon mixed spice

1 teaspoon grated nutmeg

175g (6oz) butter, softened

75g (3oz) light soft brown sugar

175g (6oz) mixed dried fruit

1 egg, beaten

A little milk for mixing

Caster sugar for dredging

Makes 12 cakes

Preheat the oven to 220°C, 425°F, gas mark 7. Grease a large baking tray. Mix together the flour, baking powder and spices. Rub in the butter, then stir in the sugar and dried fruit. Add the beaten egg and enough milk to mix to a stiff dough. Spoon on to the prepared tray and bake for 15–20 minutes until golden. Remove from the oven and dredge with caster sugar. Serve warm with butter.

Pembrokeshire Buns

The recipe for these traditional Welsh fruited buns is very similar to that for Hot Cross Buns (see page 44), leftovers of which were believed to have magical powers to protect against disease and to frighten away witches and demons. Pembrokeshire Buns were made for New Year celebrations and children would go from door to door wishing everyone a Happy New Year and each receiving a bun as a reward.

15g (½oz) lard, softened
15g (½oz) butter, softened
450g (1lb) plain flour, sifted
50g (2oz) caster sugar
50g (2oz) currants
25g (1oz) mixed candied peel
25g (1oz) fresh yeast (to substitute dried yeast, see page 11)
250ml (9fl oz) warm milk and water, mixed

Makes 11 buns

Grease two baking trays. Rub the fat into the flour. Add the sugar, currants and peel and stir well. Dissolve the yeast in the milk and water and add to the dry ingredients. Mix to a soft dough and leave in a warm place to rise for 15 minutes. On a lightly floured board, knead the dough and then divide it into eleven 75g (3oz) pieces. Roll with the hands to form round buns, place on the prepared trays and leave in a warm place for 10 minutes until well risen. Meanwhile preheat the oven to 200°C, 400°F, gas mark 6. When the buns are well risen, bake for 15–20 minutes until golden. Remove from the oven and lift on to a wire rack to cool.

Bath Buns

In the 18th century, these local treats were flavoured with sherry, rose water and caraway seeds. The more modern version uses candied citrus peel and currants and is topped with the characteristic crushed lump sugar which gives the buns their distinctive crunchy quality.

25g (1oz) fresh yeast (to substitute dried yeast, see page 11)
100g (4oz) caster sugar
550g (1lb 4oz) strong plain white flour, sifted
150ml (5fl oz) milk, warmed
Pinch of salt
175g (6oz) currants and sultanas, mixed
50g (2oz) mixed candied peel
50g (2oz) butter, melted
2 eggs, beaten

Makes 20 buns

In a medium-sized bowl, cream the yeast with 1 teaspoon of the sugar. Add 100g (4oz) of the flour and the warmed milk and mix to a thick batter. Leave in a warm place for 15–20 minutes until frothy. Mix together the remaining flour and the salt. Add the remaining caster sugar, currants, sultanas and peel. Add to the yeast mixture with the melted butter and most of the beaten egg (reserving a little for glazing) and mix to a soft dough. Knead on a floured board for 2–3 minutes until smooth. Place in a lightly floured bowl, cover with a damp cloth and leave in a warm place to rise for 1½–1¾ hours until doubled in size. Grease two baking trays. Knock back the dough and form into bun shapes, each weighing approximately 65g (2½oz). Place well apart on the prepared trays, cover with oiled cling film and leave to rise for about 30 minutes until doubled in size. Meanwhile heat the oven to 190°C, 375°F, gas mark 5. Glaze the buns with the remaining beaten egg and sprinkle with the crushed sugar. Bake for 15 minutes until well risen and golden. Remove from the oven and lift on to a wire rack to cool.

48

Chelsea Buns

London's Chelsea Buns were originally made and sold in the Old Chelsea Bun House, a bakery owned and run in Pimlico, London, by Richard Hand, who was known by most people as Captain Bun.

225g (8oz) strong plain white
    flour, sifted
15g (½oz) fresh yeast (to substitute
    dried yeast, see page 11)
1 teaspoon caster sugar
125ml (4fl oz) warm milk
15g (½oz) lard, softened
Pinch of salt

1 egg, beaten
50g (2oz) butter, melted
50g (2oz) raisins
50g (2oz) currants
50g (2oz) sultanas
25g (1oz) mixed candied peel
50g (2oz) light soft brown sugar
Honey to glaze

Makes 9 buns

Grease a 17.5cm (7in) square tin. Put 50g (2oz) of the flour into a bowl and add the yeast, caster sugar and milk. Mix to a smooth batter and leave in a warm place for 20 minutes until frothy. Rub the lard into the remaining flour. Add the salt, the yeast mixture and the beaten egg, and mix to a soft dough. Knead on a floured board for about 5 minutes until really smooth. Place in a bowl, cover with a clean, damp cloth and leave in a warm place for 1–1½ hours until doubled in size. Knead again on a floured board and then roll out to a rectangle approximately 22.5 x 30cm (9 x 12in). Brush the melted butter over the surface and sprinkle the dried fruit and sugar over, leaving a narrow border all the way round the edge. Roll up like a Swiss roll, starting with the longer side. Brush the edges of the dough with water and seal carefully. Cut the roll into nine pieces and place the rolls, cut side uppermost, in the prepared tin. Leave in a warm place for a further 30 minutes until well risen. Meanwhile heat the oven to 190°C, 375°F, gas mark 5. When the buns are risen, bake for 30–35 minutes until golden. Remove from the oven, turn out on to a wire rack and, while still warm, brush the tops with honey. To serve, pull apart and eat warm or cold.

Right: Chelsea Buns
Next page: Bath Buns

Cherry and Almond Scones

From Rufford Old Hall in Lancashire comes the recipe for scones subtly flavoured with a hint of almonds. Although it was built in the early 15th century, long before the English learnt about tea, the house has many interesting tea-related items including various unusual teapots and a large ornate 'teapoy'. Intended to double as a small tea table and as a box that contained the tea, its name does not derive from 'tea' but from Hindi tipai *meaning three-footed, since its sturdy leg usually ended in three carved feet.*

450g (1lb) self-raising flour, sifted
¼ teaspoon baking powder
100g (4oz) butter, softened
75g (3oz) caster sugar
175g (6oz) glacé cherries, roughly chopped
1 egg, beaten
A few drops of almond essence
175–200ml (6–7fl oz) milk

Makes 20 scones

Preheat the oven to 180°C, 350°F, gas mark 4. Grease two baking trays. Mix together the flour and baking powder and rub in the butter. Add the sugar, cherries, beaten egg, almond essence and enough milk to give a soft but not sticky dough. Knead lightly until smooth. On a floured board, roll out to a thickness of 1cm (½in) and cut out rounds using a 5cm (2in) cutter. Place on the prepared trays and bake for 20–25 minutes until well risen, firm and golden. Remove from the oven and lift on to a wire rack to cool. Serve with butter or clotted cream and jam.

Left: Cherry and Almond Scones
Previous page: Ginger and Treacle Scones

Ginger and Treacle Scones

From Wimpole Hall in Cambridgeshire comes this spicy, richly dark scone recipe. To ensure a regular supply of quality loose leaf tea during the years of rationing that followed World War II, the Bambridge family who lived at Wimpole Hall entrusted its entire stock of tea coupons to Twinings tea company. From 1950 to 1953 further orders for Indian tea were placed with Twinings and the tea usually arrived in 14-lb cases or sometimes in 5-lb packets. The various tea caddies displayed around the house would once have been regularly filled from a large lockable storage bin kept in the housekeeper's dry store in the basement.

225g (8oz) self-raising flour, sifted
1½ teaspoons baking powder
2 teaspoons ground ginger
50g (2oz) butter, softened and cut into small pieces
6 tablespoons milk
1 rounded tablespoon black treacle
A little milk to glaze

Makes 11 scones

Preheat the oven to 220°C, 425°F, gas mark 7. Grease a baking tray. Mix together the flour, baking powder and ginger and rub in the fat until the mixture resembles breadcrumbs. Warm the milk and treacle together in a small pan until lukewarm. Add to the mixture and mix with a round-bladed knife to a soft dough. On a lightly floured board, knead until smooth, then roll out to a thickness of 1.5cm (¾in). Cut into rounds using a 5cm (2in) cutter and place on the prepared tray. Brush the tops with a little milk. Bake just above the centre of the oven for 10–15 minutes until well risen and golden brown. Remove from the oven and lift on to a wire rack to cool. Serve warm or cold with butter.

Fruit Scones

The recipe for these scones comes from Little Moreton Hall in Cheshire which was built in the late 16th century, about 100 years before the first tea arrived in England.

450g (1lb) self-raising flour, sifted
Pinch of salt
½ teaspoon baking powder
100g (4oz) butter, softened

1½ tablespoons caster sugar
1½ tablespoons sultanas
Just under 300ml (10fl oz) milk

Makes 14–16 scones

Preheat the oven to 220°C, 425°F, gas mark 7. Grease two baking trays. Mix together the flour, salt and baking powder and rub in the butter. Add the sugar and sultanas and mix with enough milk to give a soft dough. On a floured board, roll out to a thickness of 1.5cm (¾in) and cut into rounds using a 6cm (2½in) cutter. Place on the prepared trays and bake for 13–15 minutes until golden and firm. Remove from the oven and lift on to a wire rack to cool. Serve warm or cold with butter.

Wholemeal Fruit Scones

450g (1lb) strong plain wholemeal
   flour, sifted
1 tablespoon baking powder
90g (3½oz) butter
50g (2oz) white Flora
a pinch of salt
½ teaspoon ground cinnamon

½ teaspoon grated nutmeg
50g (2oz) mixed dried fruit (such as
   currants, raisins and peel)
75g (3oz) sultanas
50g (2oz) light soft brown sugar
2 eggs
100–150ml (4–5fl oz) milk

Makes approximately 20–22 scones

Preheat the oven to 220°C, 425°F, gas mark 7. Grease two baking trays. Mix together the flour and baking powder and rub in the fats so that the mixture resembles fine breadcrumbs. Add the salt, spices, dried fruit and sugar and stir well. Beat the eggs. Add to the dry ingredients and mix with enough of the milk to give a soft dough. On a lightly floured board, pat out to a thickness of 1.5cm (¾in) and cut into rounds using a 6cm (2½in) cutter. Place on the prepared trays and bake for 15 minutes until golden brown and firm. Remove from the oven and lift on to a wire rack to cool.

Eggless Scones

The name for scones seems to descend from Dutch schoonbrot *or German* sconbrot *meaning fine bread, and they seem to have become part of afternoon tea menus in the latter half of the 19th century.*

50g (2oz) butter, softened
50g (2oz) lard, softened

350g (12oz) self-raising flour, sifted
100–115ml (4–4½fl oz) milk

Makes approximately 12 scones

Preheat the oven to 190°C, 375°F, gas mark 5. Grease two baking trays. Rub the fats into the flour, working as quickly and lightly as possible with cold hands. Add enough milk to give a soft, bread-like dough. On a floured board, roll out to a thickness of 1.5cm (¾in) and cut into rounds with a 6cm (2½in) cutter. Place on the prepared trays and bake for 15–20 minutes until lightly golden and well risen. Remove from the oven and lift on to a wire rack to cool. Despite containing no eggs, this recipe makes light, well-risen scones – perfect served warm with jam and Cornish clotted cream.

Irish Honey Scones

Should clotted cream go on the scone before or after the jam? The answer depends on where the scone is being eaten. In Devon they say that cream goes first because it is possible to get more cream to stay on the scone! In Cornwall, the cream follows the jam.

100g (4oz) plain wholemeal flour
100g (4oz) plain white flour, sifted
2 teaspoons baking powder
Pinch of salt

75g (3oz) butter, softened
1 tablespoon light soft brown sugar
2 tablespoons clear honey
50–75ml (2–3fl oz) milk

Makes 1 x 17.5cm (7in) round

Preheat the oven to 200°C, 400°F, gas mark 6. Grease a baking tray. Mix together the flour, baking powder and salt and rub in the butter. Add the sugar and mix. Mix the honey with the milk and stir until the honey has dissolved. Reserve a little for glazing and add the rest to the flour. Mix to a soft dough. Place the dough on the prepared tray and shape with the hands into a flat round approximately 17.5cm (7in) in diameter. Divide the top into eight wedges. Bake for 15–20 minutes. Remove from the oven, glaze the top with the honey and milk mixture and return to the oven for a further 5–10 minutes until golden. Remove from the oven and serve warm with butter.

Welsh Cheese and Herb Scones

Obviously not intended to be eaten with clotted cream, savoury scones make a satisfying part of high tea. This recipe comes from Penrhyn Castle in Wales which inexplicably has a Russian samovar on display. Tea traditions from around the world can generally trace their origins back to China, where tea was discovered, and the samovar is no exception. Tea was originally traded into Russia overland from northern China, through Mongolia, and the traders learnt to adapt the Mongolian cooking pot (with its central chimney and surrounding body where food is braised or simmered) to create a vessel that could both brew tea and keep the pot or tea liquor hot. Tea is brewed very strong in a small teapot which then sits on top of the central chimney until required. Half a cup of tea is then poured and topped up with hot water from the body of the samovar.

450g (1lb) self-raising flour, sifted
1 teaspoon salt
100g (4oz) butter, softened
1 teaspoon mixed dried herbs
225g (8oz) Cheddar or other strong cheese, grated
8 tablespoons milk
8 tablespoons water

Makes approximately 12 scones

Preheat the oven to 220°C, 425°F, gas mark 7. Grease a baking tray. Mix together the flour and salt and rub in the butter. Add the herbs and 175g (6oz) of the cheese. Add the milk and water and mix to a soft dough. On a floured board, roll out to a thickness of 2.5cm (1in) and cut into rounds using a 6cm (2½in) cutter. Place on the prepared tray, top each scone with a little of the remaining grated cheese and bake for 10 minutes until golden. Remove from the oven and lift on to a wire rack to cool slightly. Serve warm or cold with butter.

Stiffkey Cakes

This recipe comes from Norfolk's Blickling Hall whose kitchen often has two sugar cones on display. Sugar was always purchased in solid cones of different sizes and had to be chopped into smaller pieces with wrought-iron choppers and tongs. When tea arrived in England in the late 1650s, it was advertised and drunk as a medicinal herb and, since herbal tonics had always been sweetened with molasses, honey or sugar, tea was drunk in the same way. For the tea table, small pieces were arranged on a porcelain dish and served with elegant silver tongs.

350g (12oz) plain flour, sifted
1 teaspoon baking powder
25g (1oz) butter, softened
25g (1oz) caster sugar
2 eggs, beaten
A few drops of lemon essence or the juice of half a lemon
Caster sugar for dredging

Makes 8 cakes

Preheat the oven to 200°C, 400°F, gas mark 6. Grease a baking tray. Mix together the flour and baking powder and rub in the fat. Add the sugar and mix well. Add the beaten eggs and lemon essence or juice and mix to a soft dough. On a floured board, roll out to a thickness of 2.5cm (1in) and cut into rounds using a 6cm (2½in) cutter. Place on the prepared tray and bake for 15 minutes until pale golden. Remove from the oven and lift carefully on to a wire rack to cool. Dredge with caster sugar before serving.

These cakes are rather like scones and were made in the 1860s by a local woman in Norfolk called Peggy Muns. Stiffkey on the north Norfolk coast is also famous for its dark shelled cockles, known locally as Stewkey Blues.

Devon Flats

An important traditional ingredient in these little biscuits is Devonshire clotted cream which is today manufactured in commercial dairies. But before mechanization, it was made in the individual dairy of each large farm or country house where fresh, creamy milk was left to stand for 24 hours to settle. It was then gently heated until a thick layer of cream formed on the surface and was skimmed off ready to be eaten piled on to puddings, desserts and freshly baked scones.

225g (8oz) self-raising flour, sifted
Pinch of salt
100g (4oz) caster sugar
100ml (4fl oz) clotted or double cream
1 egg, beaten
1 tablespoon fresh milk

Makes 24 flats

Preheat the oven to 220°C, 425°F, gas mark 7. Grease two baking trays. Mix together the flour, salt and sugar. Add the cream, beaten egg and enough milk to give a stiff dough. On a lightly floured board, roll out to a thickness of approximately 0.75cm (⅜in) and cut into circles using a 7.5cm (3in) cutter. Place on the prepared trays and bake for 8–10 minutes until golden. Remove from the oven and lift carefully on to a wire rack to cool.

Sally Lunns

Some say that these soft, slightly sweet cakes are named after the girl who sold them in the streets of Bath in the 18th century. Others suggest that the name derives from the French soleil lune *because the tops of the Sally Lunns are golden like the sun and the base is pale like the moon. It is customary to split the freshly baked, warm cakes and fill them with cream and jam but they make an excellent alternative to bread for favourite savoury sandwich fillings.*

25g (1oz) fresh yeast (to substitute dried yeast, see page 11)
2 teaspoons caster sugar
2 eggs, beaten
300ml (10fl oz) double cream
450g (1lb) plain flour, sifted
Pinch of salt
Warm water for mixing

Makes 1 large flat cake or 5–6 small round cakes

Cream together the yeast and sugar and mix with the beaten eggs and cream. Mix together the flour and salt. Add the yeast mixture and mix with enough warm water to give a light dough. Leave in the bowl in a warm place for 1½ hours until doubled in size. Grease a baking tray. Turn the dough on to a floured board and knead lightly. Shape into one large flat cake or five or six small ones and place on the tray. Leave in a warm place for a further 20–30 minutes until well risen. Meanwhile heat the oven to 200°C, 400°F, gas mark 6. When the cakes are well risen, bake for 20–25 minutes until golden. Remove from the oven, tear open and spread with thick cream or butter. Put back together and serve immediately.

Cornish Splits

Eaten as an alternative to scones, the recipe for these splits comes from Lanhydrock, originally built in the 17th century but partly destroyed by fire and rebuilt in the 19th. Cooks and maids in its vast kitchens would have busied themselves regularly making bread, splits, cakes and biscuits to satisfy the family's teatime requirements. In the morning room each day, a table is covered with a lace cloth and set ready for tea with French china tea cups and saucers, silver tea knives and teaspoons, small linen napkins, a beehive honey pot, a silver jam pot and a silver butter dish.

50g (2oz) fresh yeast (to substitute dried yeast, see page 11)
40g (1½oz) caster sugar
Just under 600ml (1 pint) warm milk and water mixed
900g (2lb) strong plain white flour, sifted
1 egg, beaten

Makes 12 splits

Grease two baking trays. Mix together the yeast, sugar and warm milk and water. Leave in a warm place for about 20–30 minutes until frothy. Add the liquid to the flour with the beaten egg and mix to a soft dough. Knead until smooth and elastic. Leave in a warm place for about an hour until doubled in size. Knock back, knead again and divide into 75g (3oz) pieces. Mould with the hands into neat bun shapes, place on the prepared trays and leave in a warm place for about 20 minutes until well risen. Meanwhile heat the oven to 160°C, 325°F, gas mark 3. When the splits are well risen, bake for 20–25 minutes until they just start to turn brown. Remove from the oven and cool on a wire rack. To serve, split and fill with jam and clotted cream and dust the tops with icing sugar.

Singin' Hinny

The north-east of England has retained many of its traditional recipes and this is a favourite larded dough that hisses or sings as the fat sizzles during the baking. It is one of those scrummy foods that we all know is bad for us, but occasionally we need to indulge in to relive the past!

350g (12oz) self-raising flour, sifted
1 teaspoon baking powder
50g (2oz) ground rice
1 teaspoon salt
50g (2oz) butter, softened
50g (2oz) caster sugar
75g (3oz) currants
150ml (5fl oz) double cream
150ml (5fl oz) milk

Makes 1 x 22.5cm (9in) round cake

Preheat a griddle or a large, heavy frying pan to an even, moderate temperature. Mix together the flour, baking powder, ground rice and salt and rub in the butter until the mixture resembles fine breadcrumbs. Add the sugar and currants and mix well. Add the cream and milk and mix to a stiff dough. Knead lightly until smooth. On a lightly floured board, roll out to a circle 22.5cm (9in) in diameter and about 0.5cm (¼in) in thickness. Place on the griddle or pan and cook for 4–5 minutes on each side until golden. Serve hot or cold, cut into wedges and spread with butter and jam.

Scarborough Muffins

*Muffins have been a favourite for breakfast and tea since Victorian times. They were once
the food of the servants who worked and ate 'below stairs' in large Victorian mansions and
the original recipes involved a mixture of leftover bread scraps and potatoes which were fried
on a griddle. Gradually, they made their way upstairs on to breakfast and tea tables in smart
dining and drawing rooms and 'muffin men' would hawk them in the street attracting
customers by ringing a loud bell as they walked through the town with their tray of muffins
balanced on their heads. Each region has its own recipe and this one makes a light, soft
sponge that is excellent with cheese or preserves.*

400g (14oz) plain flour, sifted
Pinch of salt
300ml (10fl oz) milk
**15g (½oz) fresh yeast (to substitute
   dried yeast, see page 11)**
1 egg

Makes 10 muffins

Grease two baking trays. Mix together the flour and salt. Warm the milk and stir into the yeast. Beat
the egg and add to the milk. Pour into the flour and blend well to give a soft dough. Knead lightly.
On a floured board, roll out to a thickness of 1cm (½in) and cut into round cakes with a 7.5cm (3in)
cutter. Place on the prepared trays and leave in a warm place for 1 hour until well risen. Meanwhile
heat the oven to 200°C, 400°F, gas mark 6. When the muffins are well risen, bake for 10 minutes
until golden. Remove from the oven and serve hot or warm with butter.

Tarts and Flans

The British love their pastry and over the centuries have filled short and flaky pastry cases with creamy egg custards, lemon and curd cheese mixtures, buttery and spiced dried fruit blends and whatever fresh fruits are in season. As well as featuring on the tea table, many of these recipes can double as desserts served with whipped cream or delicious, velvety custard.

Norfolk Tart

Norfolk is more famous for its use of honey in desserts and cakes than for syrup tarts but this syrup and cream based recipe makes a teatime treat. Honey has been a local product in the county for hundreds of years, especially at Walsingham where the monks kept colonies of bees.

175g (6oz) rich shortcrust pastry (see page 15)
100g (4oz) golden syrup
15g (½oz) butter
Grated rind of half a lemon
2 tablespoons double cream
1 egg

Makes 1 x 17.5cm (7in) round tart

Make the pastry according to the instructions on page 15 and chill for at least 15 minutes. Preheat the oven to 200°C, 400°F, gas mark 6. Grease a 17.5cm (7in) round flan tin or dish. On a floured board, roll out the pastry to make a circle and use to line the prepared tin or dish. Bake blind for 15–20 minutes. Remove from the oven and lift out the baking beans and paper. Reduce the oven temperature to 180°C, 350°F, gas mark 4. Warm the syrup in a pan with the butter and lemon rind until the butter has dissolved. Beat the cream and egg together and add to the mixture. Pour into the pastry case and bake for 20 minutes until golden and firm. Remove from the oven and serve warm or cold.

This delicious traditional tart is ideal served at teatime or as a dessert with whipped or clotted cream.

Manchester Tart

This meringue-topped tart is a little like a Queen of Puddings in a pastry shell. The recipe comes from Dunham Massey in Cheshire where the 'tearoom' in the house holds rare tea and coffee tables, the family silver teawares and two tall tea caddies of japanned metal inlaid with mother of pearl. These large tins would have held the main supply of loose-leaf tea and smaller caddies, now on show on side tables and mantel shelves in the drawing and dining rooms, would have been regularly replenished.

175g (6oz) flaky pastry (see page 14)
3–4 tablespoons raspberry or strawberry jam
Rind of 1 lemon, cut into strips
300ml (10fl oz) milk
50g (2oz) fresh breadcrumbs
50g (2oz) butter, softened
2 eggs, separated
75g (3oz) caster sugar
1 tablespoon brandy
Caster sugar for dredging

Makes 1 x 20cm (8in) round tart

Make the pastry according to the instructions on page 14 and chill for at least 45 minutes. Preheat the oven to 190°C, 375°F, gas mark 5. Grease and line an 20cm (8in) round pie dish or loose-bottomed round tin. On a floured board, roll out the pastry and use to line the prepared tin. Spread the jam over the base. Put the lemon rind and milk into a pan and bring to the boil. Remove from the heat and strain on to the breadcrumbs. Leave to stand for 5 minutes. Add the butter, egg yolks, 25g (1oz) of the sugar and the brandy and beat well. Pour into the pastry case and bake for 45 minutes. Meanwhile whisk the egg whites until stiff and fold in the remaining 50g (2oz) of the sugar. Remove the tart from the oven and spread the meringue over the filling. Dredge with caster sugar and bake for a further 15 minutes until the meringue is brown. Remove from the oven and leave to cool. Serve cold with cream.

Lancaster Lemon Tart

Today we take afternoon tea at 4 or 5 o'clock but in the early days of tea drinking in England, tea was served as an after-dinner 'digestif'. When the last morsels of food had been consumed, the company would retire to a drawing room where the tea table had been prepared by the servants. The lady of the house would set the silver kettle to boil, take her porcelain or silver tea jar from the shelf, warm the little Chinese porcelain or earthenware teapot, then measure in the correct amount of tea and pour on the boiling water. She would then pour the brew into tiny, handleless Chinese porcelain bowls and hand them around to her family and friends.

175g (6oz) shortcrust pastry (see page 16)
150–175g (5–6oz) lemon curd
100g (4oz) butter, softened
100g (4oz) caster sugar
2 eggs, beaten
3 teaspoons lemon juice
75g (3oz) self-raising flour, sifted
25g (1oz) ground almonds

Makes 1 x 20cm (8in) round tart

Make the pastry according to the instructions on page 16 and chill for at least 15 minutes. Preheat the oven to 180°C, 350°F, gas mark 4. Grease a 20cm (8in) loose-bottomed round flan tin. On a floured board, roll out the pastry and use to line the tin. Spread the lemon curd over the base. Beat together the butter and sugar until pale and fluffy. Gradually add the beaten eggs and the lemon juice and beat well. Add the flour and ground almonds and fold in with a metal spoon. Spread the mixture over the lemon curd and smooth out. Bake for 35 minutes, then reduce the oven temperature to 150°C, 300°F, gas mark 2 and bake for 10–15 minutes more until the sponge springs back when lightly pressed. Remove from the oven and leave to cool in the tin. When cold, cut into pieces.

Right: Lancaster Lemon Tart
Next page: Manchester Tart

Spicy Apple Flan

Suffolk was once an important apple-growing region, with orchards mainly found in the east and south of the county. Most of the apple producers owned smallholdings and sent their crop to the London markets by rail or road. The most famous of the local apples is the St Edmund's Russet, named for Saint Edmund, Saxon king of the East Angles in the 9th century AD.

FOR THE BASE
175g (6oz) self-raising flour, sifted
100g (4oz) butter, softened
1 egg, beaten
40g (1½oz) granulated or light or dark soft brown sugar
Pinch of salt

FOR THE TOPPING
5 large cooking apples, peeled, cored and sliced
50g (2oz) sugar
1 teaspoon mixed spice
50g (2oz) sultanas

Makes 8 portions

Preheat the oven to 180°C, 350°F, gas mark 4. Grease a 17.5cm (7in) round tin. Using a fork or electric beater, mix together the ingredients for the base and, on a lightly floured board, roll out to make a circle to fit the tin. Place in the tin and press well against the edges. Arrange the apples in layers on top of the dough, sprinkling some of the sugar, spice and sultanas on each layer. Bake for 1 hour, watching carefully, until the top is browned and the apples are tender. Remove from the oven and leave to cool in the tin.

Left: Spicy Apple Flan
Previous page: Cherry Bakewells

Cherry Bakewells

Bakewell tarts descend from what were originally called Bakewell puddings, said to date back to the 16th century and to have been invented by accident when a cook at a local inn misunderstood her employee's instructions to make a strawberry tart. Apparently, instead of adding eggs and sugar to the pastry, she beat them up with a secret ingredient and spread the mixture over the strawberries. Today, the recipe calls for strawberry jam instead of fresh fruit and sometimes decorates the top with a little icing and a cherry.

225g (8oz) shortcrust pastry (see page 16)
50g (2oz) strawberry jam
100g (4oz) butter, softened
100g (4oz) caster sugar
2 eggs
50g (2oz) ground almonds
50g (2oz) self-raising four, sifted
1 teaspoon almond essence
175g (6oz) icing sugar, sifted
1–2 tablespoons water
20 cherries (fresh, stoned or glacé)

Makes 20 tarts

Make the pastry according to the instructions on page 16 and chill for at least 15 minutes. Preheat the oven to 200°C, 400°F, gas mark 6. Grease 20 patty tins. On a lightly floured board, roll out the pastry and cut twenty circles using a 7.5cm (3in) cutter. Use to line the prepared tins and spread a little jam in the base of each. Beat together the fat and caster sugar, then beat in the eggs, one at a time, adding half the ground almonds after each one. Add the flour and almond essence and stir well. Spoon the mixture into the pastry cases and bake for 20 minutes until well risen, firm and golden. Remove from the oven and leave to cool in the tins. Mix together the icing sugar and water and, when the tarts are cold, spoon the icing on to the top. Decorate each with a cherry.

Wilfra Apple Cake

One of Yorkshire's best-known pastries, this was baked in Ripon on St Wilfrid's Day (the first or second Saturday of August) to celebrate the return of the saint to his home town after a long absence abroad. Another favourite for the same festivity were little Wilfra Tarts which the residents of the town would make by the dozen and place outside their front doors so that passers-by could help themselves.

450g (1lb) shortcrust pastry (see page 16)
900g (2lb) cooking apples, peeled, cored and sliced
75–100g (3–4oz) granulated, demerara or soft brown sugar
50–75g (2–3oz) Wensleydale cheese, grated
Milk or beaten egg to glaze

Makes 1 x 17.5 x 27.5cm (7 x 11in) tart

Make the pastry according to the instructions on page 16 and chill for at least 15 minutes. Preheat the oven to 190°C, 375°F, gas mark 5. Grease a 17.5 x 27.5cm (7 x 11in) Swiss roll tin. Cook the apples gently in a pan with the sugar until just soft. On a floured board, roll out half the pastry to make a rectangle to fit the tin and use to line the base and sides. Pour in the apples and spread evenly. Sprinkle the cheese over the apples. Roll out the remaining pastry and place on top of the cheese. Brush the edges with a little milk and seal well. Brush the top with milk or beaten egg and bake for 30–35 minutes until golden. Remove from the oven and allow to cool in the tin. When cold, cut into slabs and lift carefully from the tin.

Yorkshire Curd Tart

Open curd cheese tarts and cheesecakes have been favourite puddings in Yorkshire for centuries and were often served as Easter specialities to use up some of the plentiful eggs and curd cheese available after the Lenten fast.

175g (6oz) shortcrust pastry (see page 16)
50g (2oz) butter, softened
50g (2oz) caster sugar
1 egg, beaten
50g (2oz) currants
100g (4oz) cottage cheese
50g (2oz) sponge or biscuit crumbs
Grated rind and juice of 1 lemon
½ teaspoon grated nutmeg

Makes 1 x 20cm (8in) round tart

Make the pastry according to the instructions on page 16 and chill for at least 15 minutes. Preheat the oven to 190°C, 375°F, gas mark 5. Grease a 20cm (8in) round flan dish or tin. On a floured board, roll out the pastry to make a circle to fit the prepared tin or dish and use to line the base and sides. Beat together the butter and sugar until light and fluffy. Add the beaten egg and beat hard. Add the currants, cottage cheese, sponge or biscuit crumbs, lemon rind and juice and the nutmeg and beat again. Turn into the pastry case, smooth and bake for 20–25 minutes until golden. Remove from the oven and serve warm or cold with thick cream.

Longshaw Tart

Named after the estate near Sheffield where this recipe comes from, the tart is a version of Bakewell tart, another local speciality. This may well have featured on the 'high tea' table when the family arrived home hungry at the end of the working day. Whereas 'afternoon tea' was also called 'low tea' (because one sat in low armchairs and chaise longues) or 'handed tea' (because the cups of tea were handed around by the hostess), 'high tea' was called 'meat tea' and 'great tea'.

350g (12oz) shortcrust pastry (see page 16)
6–7 tablespoons jam (raspberry, strawberry or apricot)
250g (9oz) butter, softened
250g (9oz) granulated sugar
115g (4½oz) peanuts, finely chopped
115g (4½oz) fresh breadcrumbs (white or wholemeal)
3 eggs, beaten
1½ teaspoons almond essence

Makes 20 slices

Make the pastry according to the instructions on page 16 and chill for at least 15 minutes. Preheat the oven to 190°C, 375°F, gas mark 5. Grease a 25 x 30 x 3.5cm (10 x 12 x 1½in) tin. On a floured board, roll out the pastry to make a rectangle to fit the tin and use to line the base. Spread the jam over the pastry. Beat together the butter and sugar until light and fluffy. Add the peanuts, breadcrumbs, beaten eggs and almond essence and mix well. Turn into the pastry case and bake for 25–30 minutes until firm and golden. Remove from the oven and leave to cool in the tin. When cold, cut into slices and lift carefully out of the tin.

Lakeland Coconut Tart

Instead of the almonds used in the frangipani topping for Bakewell tart and the peanuts in Longshaw tart (see page 69), this pastry-based teatime treat includes coconut. The recipe comes from Quarry Bank Mill in Cheshire which thrived as a result of the burgeoning cotton industry of the 18th century and provided schools and apprenticeship houses for the children who made up a third of the workforce. The staple diet of an average worker was potatoes and wheaten bread, washed down with tea or coffee. The Comte de la Rochefoucauld, while touring in England in 1784, wrote, 'Throughout the whole of England the drinking of tea is general. You have it twice a day and though the expense is considerable, the humblest peasant has his tea twice a day just like the rich man'.

175g (6oz) shortcrust pastry (see page 16)
3–4 tablespoons strawberry or raspberry jam
100g (4oz) butter
50g (2oz) caster sugar
2 level tablespoons golden syrup
225g (8oz) shredded coconut
2 eggs, beaten

Makes 1 x 20cm (8in) round tart

Make the pastry according to the instructions on page 16 and chill for at least 15 minutes. Preheat the oven to 190°C, 375°F, gas mark 5. Grease a 20cm (8in) round flan tin or a deep pie plate. On a floured board, roll out the pastry and use to line the prepared tin. Spread the jam over the pastry base. Melt together the butter, sugar and syrup and stir in the coconut and beaten eggs. Turn into the pastry case and bake in the middle of the oven for 30 minutes until golden (this tart browns and burns easily, so cover with foil after the first 10 minutes of baking time). Remove from the oven and leave to cool in the tin.

Treacle Tart

Beningbrough Hall near York serves this sticky, indulgent tart in its tearoom. The house, built in 1716, has a closet on the ground floor as part of a grand suite of rooms used by honoured guests. Always richly decorated, the closet was often used to entertain visitors to tea and all the essential porcelain teapots, bowls and dishes required to brew and serve tea were displayed on shelves and stepped ledges over the fireplace. The tea was too expensive to leave in charge of the servants so it was also kept here in little porcelain jars imported from China. The jars gradually changed shape and became squat, hinge-lidded caddies.

FOR THE PASTRY
50g (2oz) lard or other shortening, softened
50g (2oz) butter, softened
225g (8oz) plain flour, sifted
25g (1oz) caster sugar
A little cold water

FOR THE FILLING
450g (1lb) golden syrup
100–175g (4–6oz) fresh white breadcrumbs
Juice of half a lemon

Makes 12 portions

Make the pastry by rubbing the fats into the flour. Add the sugar and enough water to mix to a soft but pliable dough. Knead lightly, wrap in foil or cling film and chill for at least 15 minutes. Preheat the oven to 180°C, 350°F, gas mark 4. Grease a 30cm (12in) round flan dish. On a floured board, roll out the pastry to fit the prepared dish and use to line the base and sides. Place the syrup in a pan and warm gently. Remove from the heat, add the breadcrumbs and lemon juice and leave until the bread is well soaked. If the mixture is dry, add a little more syrup. Turn the mixture into the pastry case and spread evenly. Bake for 25–30 minutes until the pastry is golden and the filling nicely browned. Remove from the oven and serve warm or cold.

Secretary Tarts

These oddly named tartlets are served in the tearoom at Polesden Lacey in Surrey – a Regency house with strong links to afternoon tea rituals. Hosted by Mrs Ronnie Greville, the elegant but renowned society hostess, tea was an important part of the famous parties held from 1906 until the outbreak of World War II. Guests included Indian maharajahs, literary figures such as Beverley Nichols and Harold Nicolson, prominent politicians and royalty, including Edward VII and the honeymooning future George VI and Queen Elizabeth. In Down the Kitchen Sink, *Beverley Nichols noted, 'Tea is at 5 o'clock – and not 5 minutes past – which means that the Spanish ambassador, who has gone for a walk down the yew avenue, hastily retraces his steps, and that the Chancellor of the Exchequer … hurries down the great staircase, and that various gentlemen rise from their chaise longues … and join the procession to the tearoom. The teapots, the cream jugs, the milk pots and the sugar basins are Queen Anne silver; the tea service is Meissen; and the doyleys, heavily monogrammed, are of Chantilly lace'.*

450g (1lb) rich shortcrust or shortcrust pastry (see page 15 or 16)
175g (6oz) butter
175g (6oz) light soft brown sugar
1 x 405g (14oz) large can condensed milk
50g (2oz) walnuts, roughly chopped
50g (2oz) raisins

Makes 24 tarts

Make the pastry according to the instructions on page 15 or 16 and chill for at least 15 minutes. Preheat the oven to 230°C, 450°F, gas mark 8. Grease 24 patty tins. On a floured board, roll out the pastry to a thickness of 0.5cm (¼in) and cut 24 circles using a 7.5cm (3in) fluted cutter. Use to line the prepared patty tins. Place little squares of greaseproof paper in each tart and fill with baking beans. Bake blind for 10 minutes. Remove from the oven, lift the baking beans and paper out of the cases and return to the oven for a further 5 minutes. Remove and turn off the oven. Put the butter, sugar and milk into a medium-sized pan and bring to the boil. Boil hard for 7 minutes, stirring all the time, until the mixture becomes a caramel colour. Remove from the heat and allow to cool for 5 minutes. Stir in the walnuts and raisins and spoon into the pastry cases. Put into the refrigerator to set.

Kentish Pudding Pies

These little tarts are typical of the cheesecakes and egg custards that were popular in England as far back as the 17th century. Until the 19th century, eggs, like all animal products, were forbidden during the Lenten fast. The hens of course went on laying during Lent, and the surplus of eggs was used over the Easter weekend in egg custards and tarts. In Kent these would be eaten with cherry beer – ale with cherry juice added.

450g (1lb) shortcrust pastry (see page 16)
600ml (1 pint) milk
3 strips of lemon rind
100g (4oz) butter
75g (3oz) caster sugar
2 eggs, beaten
50g (2oz) ground rice
Pinch of salt
Juice of half a lemon
50g (2oz) currants

Makes 24 tarts

Make the pastry according to the instructions on page 16 and chill for 15 minutes. Put the milk and lemon rind in a pan and stand it over a gentle heat for about 20 minutes. Meanwhile preheat the oven to 180°C, 350°F, gas mark 4. Grease 24 patty tins. On a floured board, roll out the pastry to a thickness of 0.5cm (¼in) and cut 24 circles using a 7.5cm (3in) cutter. Line the prepared patty tins with the pastry circles. Remove the strips of lemon rind from the milk and discard. Add the butter and 50g (2oz) of the sugar to the milk and stir well. Mix together the beaten eggs, the ground rice, salt and lemon juice and add to the saucepan. Stir over a gentle heat until the mixture begins to thicken. Stir in the currants. Spoon the mixture into the pastry cases and sprinkle with the remaining sugar. Bake for 25–30 minutes until the pastry is golden and the filling is firm and well risen. Remove from the oven and leave to cool in the tins.

Maids of Honour

Surrey's Maids of Honour started life at Hampton Court in the days of Henry VIII. According to legend, one day the king came across some of Anne Boleyn's maids enjoying some little tartlets and asked if he could try one. He declared it so good that the recipe must be kept only for royal consumption. Then in the reign of George I, it is said that a lady at court gave the secret recipe to a gentleman who set up shop in Richmond where he baked and sold the tarts. In 1951, the recipe was made public.

450g (1lb) rich shortcrust pastry (see page 15)
100g (4oz) curd cheese
75g (3oz) butter, softened
2 eggs, beaten
65ml (2½fl oz) brandy
75g (3oz) caster sugar
75g (3oz) cold mashed potatoes
25g (1oz) ground almonds
½ teaspoon grated nutmeg
Grated rind of 2 lemons
Juice of 1 lemon

Makes approximately 24 tarts

Make the pastry according to the instructions on page 15 and chill for at least 15 minutes. Preheat the oven to 180°C, 350°F, gas mark 4. Grease 24 patty tins. On a lightly floured board, roll out the pastry and cut 24 circles using a 7.5cm (3in) cutter. Use to line the prepared patty tins. Beat together the curd cheese and butter. Add the beaten eggs, brandy and sugar and beat again. In a separate bowl beat together the mashed potatoes, ground almonds, nutmeg, lemon rind and juice, and gradually mix in the cheese mixture. Beat thoroughly. Spoon into the pastry cases and bake for 35–40 minutes until risen, golden and firm. Remove from the oven and leave to cool in the tins for 5–10 minutes before lifting carefully on to a wire rack to finish cooling.

Sly Cake

Several of Yorkshire's local specialities have acquired odd names over the centuries. Yorkshire Moggie is a kind of gingerbread, Stottie cake is a flat bread, and Sly cake fills a flat pastry case with dried fruits, walnuts, sugar and butter. Although foreign visitors may attempt to eat such sticky sweetmeats with knife and fork at teatime, British etiquette demands that we use either a pastry fork, held in the right hand, or our fingers, perhaps assisted by a small tea knife. We never use both together at teatime.

350–400g (12–14oz) shortcrust pastry (see page 16)
175g (6oz) stoned dates, chopped
50g (2oz) raisins
50g (2oz) currants
50g (2oz) walnuts, chopped
50g (2oz) light or dark soft brown sugar
4 tablespoons water
50g (2oz) butter
1–2 tablespoons milk
2 tablespoons demerara sugar for dredging

Makes 8–10 pieces

Make the pastry according to the instructions on page 16 and chill for at least 15 minutes. Preheat the oven to 190°C, 375°F, gas mark 5. Grease a tin measuring approximately 10 x 22.5cm (4 x 9in). On a floured board, roll out half the pastry and use to line the base and sides of the tin. Put the dates, raisins, currants, walnuts, sugar, water and butter into a pan, bring to the boil and simmer for 10 minutes. Remove from the heat and allow to cool for a few minutes. Turn the mixture into the pastry case and spread evenly. Roll out the remaining pastry and lay over the fruit. Dampen the edges of the pastry with a little milk and pinch well together. Brush the top with milk, dredge with the demerara sugar and bake for 25–30 minutes until the pastry is golden. Remove from the oven and leave to cool in the tin. When cold, cut into pieces and remove carefully from the tin.

Biscuits

Favourite crunchy fairings and cookies, and soft, crumbly shortbreads often have historic connections to pagan celebrations, fairs, high days and holidays. Today, these quick and easy-to-make recipes offer a satisfying alternative to shop-bought teatime nibbles.

Cornish Fairings

At fairgrounds in the past, travelling salesmen often sold little bags of delicacies containing such things as spiced biscuits, caraway comfits, candied angelica, macaroons and almond sweetmeats. Gradually, over the years, the cakes and biscuits were sold as separate items and became known as fairings.

100g (4oz) butter
100g (4oz) granulated sugar
100g (4oz) golden syrup
225g (8oz) plain flour, sifted
1 teaspoon baking powder
1 teaspoon bicarbonate of soda
1 teaspoon ground ginger
1 teaspoon mixed spice
1 teaspoon ground cinnamon

Makes approximately 26 biscuits

Preheat the oven to 150°C, 300°F, gas mark 2. Grease two or three baking trays. Put the butter, sugar and syrup into a small pan and melt gently together until the sugar is dissolved. Mix together the dry ingredients and add the sugar mixture. Mix to a soft dough. Form the dough into balls weighing approximately 22g (¾oz) and place on the prepared trays, leaving plenty of room for the biscuits to spread while cooking. Press each ball down lightly and bake for 10–15 minutes until golden. Remove from the oven and leave to cool on the trays for 5 minutes before lifting carefully on to a wire rack to cool completely.

Abbeys

Sometimes the enjoyment of a cup of tea is enhanced by the addition of a small sweet treat and these biscuits are perfect. With their chocolate coating, they combine well with a strong tea such as Kenya, Assam or a robust English Breakfast. English breakfast blends are usually made up of a mixture of teas from Assam in north-east India, Ceylon from the southern central mountains of the island of Sri Lanka, and African teas from Kenya or Malawi.

FOR THE BISCUITS
100g (4oz) butter, softened
100g (4oz) caster sugar
1 teaspoon golden syrup
100g (4oz) self-raising flour, sifted
100g (4oz) porridge oats
½ tablespoon full-cream milk powder (Coffeemate or similar)
¼ teaspoon bicarbonate of soda

FOR THE COATING
275g (10oz) plain or milk chocolate

Makes 16 biscuits

Preheat the oven to 150°C, 300°F, gas mark 2. Grease two baking trays. Beat together the butter, sugar and syrup until light and fluffy. Add the other ingredients and work together. Form the mixture into balls weighing approximately 25g (1oz) and place on the prepared trays. Press down slightly with the palm of the hand and bake for 20 minutes until pale golden. Remove from the oven and leave to cool on the trays for a few minutes before lifting on to a wire rack to cool completely. Melt the chocolate in a narrow but deep container (a cup or small bowl) and dip the biscuits into the chocolate so that half of each biscuit is coated. Place carefully on the wire rack or on greaseproof paper and leave to set.

These are excellent served with ice-cream or other light desserts, as well as being perfect with morning coffee or afternoon tea.

Easter Biscuits

A little like shortbread, Easter biscuits are a West Country traditional speciality. It is said that bakers in the past added the bitter herb tansy to represent Christ's suffering on the cross and this is sometimes replicated with lemon peel today.

FOR THE BISCUITS
175g (6oz) plain flour, sifted
50g (2oz) rice flour
1 teaspoon mixed spice
100g (4oz) butter, softened
100g (4oz) caster sugar
2 egg yolks
75g (3oz) currants
1 tablespoon brandy
½ tablespoon milk

FOR THE TOPPING
2 egg whites, lightly beaten
2 tablespoons caster sugar

Makes 10 biscuits

Preheat the oven to 180°C, 350°F, gas mark 4. Grease two baking trays. Mix together the flour, rice flour and mixed spice. Beat together the butter and sugar until light and fluffy. Beat in the egg yolks, one at a time. Add the currants, flour mixture, brandy and milk and mix to a stiff dough. Turn on to a lightly floured board and knead gently until smooth. Roll out to a thickness of 0.5cm (¼in) and cut into rounds using a 10cm (4in) fluted cutter. Place on the prepared trays and brush with plenty of beaten egg white. Sprinkle with caster sugar and bake for 15–20 minutes until crisp and pale golden. Remove from the oven and leave to cool on the trays for 5 minutes before lifting carefully on to a wire rack to cool completely.

These are light biscuits with a subtle spice and brandy flavour and a delicious crunchy topping.

Right: Easter Biscuits

Peanut and Orange Cookies

These crunchy little biscuits that combine peanuts, orange rind, syrup and oats are lovely with Ceylon tea. Ceylon has a bright, brisk flavour that is particularly suited to fruit and nut flavours and makes an excellent accompaniment to favourite teatime foods. Ceylon has been producing tea since the 1870s when tea plants replaced the coffee bushes which failed due to the 'coffee rust' fungus.

100g (4oz) butter
75g (3oz) light soft brown sugar
25g (1oz) golden syrup
1 tablespoon crunchy peanut butter
100g (4oz) self-raising flour, sifted
50g (2oz) rolled oats
Grated rind of 1 orange
25g (1oz) salted peanuts, chopped

Makes approximately 18 cookies

Preheat the oven to 160°C, 325°F, gas mark 3. Grease two baking trays. Put the butter, sugar, syrup and peanut butter into a small pan and heat gently until melted. Mix together the flour, oats and orange rind and make a well in the centre. Pour in the melted ingredients and mix thoroughly. Form dessertspoonfuls of the mixture into balls and place on the prepared trays, leaving sufficient room for the biscuits to spread. Press flat with the palm of the hand and sprinkle the tops with the chopped peanuts. Bake for 15–20 minutes until pale golden. Remove from the oven and leave to cool on the trays for a few minutes before lifting carefully on to a wire rack to cool completely.

Left: Peanut and Orange Cookies

Linzer Biscuits

Originally from Linz in Austria, these spiced biscuits were traditionally made with almonds and lemon. Two biscuits are sandwiched together with jam (always blackcurrant in the past but today more commonly raspberry or apricot) and sometimes the lower layer was covered with a lattice top or the hole was only cut in the top biscuit, allowing the rich colour of the jammy middle to show through.

275g (10oz) self-raising flour, sifted
Generous pinch of ground cinnamon
Generous pinch of ground cloves
225g (8oz) butter, softened
175g (6oz) caster sugar
1 egg, beaten
5–6 tablespoons raspberry or apricot jam

Makes approximately 25 double biscuits

Preheat the oven to 160°C, 325°F, gas mark 3. Grease two or three baking trays. Mix together all the ingredients except the jam to make a soft dough. Knead gently until smooth. Roll out on a floured board to a thickness of 0.5cm (¼in) and cut out circles using a 5cm (2in) cutter. Using an apple corer or a very small cutter, cut a small circle from the middle of each round and re-roll the dough to make more biscuits. Place on the prepared trays, allowing space for the biscuits to spread, and bake for 10–15 minutes until golden. Remove from the oven and leave to cool on the trays for 5 minutes before lifting on to a wire rack to cool completely. When cold, sandwich together with the jam and store in an airtight container for 1–2 days before eating.

If you don't have time to roll and cut the dough, form the mixture into balls and place on the trays. Flatten with the prongs of a fork and don't worry about making the hole in the middle.

Melting Moments

Everyone seems to have their own favourite recipe for these – sometimes made with peanuts or cornflakes, or flavoured with lemon. This one uses coconut and vanilla and is excellent accompanied by Darjeeling tea or a fragrant oolong from Taiwan or China, drunk without milk.

150g (5oz) sugar
175g (6oz) butter, softened
225g (8oz) plain flour, sifted
3 teaspoons baking powder
40g (1½oz) shredded coconut
1 teaspoon vanilla essence
10 glacé cherries, halved

Makes 20 biscuits

Preheat the oven to 160°C, 325°F, gas mark 3. Grease two baking trays. Beat together the sugar and butter until light and fluffy. Add the flour, baking powder, coconut and vanilla essence and mix thoroughly. Form the mixture into balls weighing approximately 25g (1oz) each and place on the prepared trays, leaving plenty of room for the biscuits to spread. Flatten with the palm of the hand and place a half cherry in the middle of each. Bake for 15–20 minutes until golden. Remove from the oven and leave to cool on the trays for 5 minutes before lifting on to a wire rack to cool completely.

Orange Crisps

Oranges came originally from China and are thought to have been cultivated there since around 2500 BC. By the 12th century AD, they had found their way to southern Europe and in 1493, Christopher Columbus carried the seeds from the Canary Islands to North America. The citrus tang of the juice and zest makes these little biscuits irresistible.

100g (5oz) butter, softened
150g (5oz) caster or granulated sugar
1 egg yolk
225g (8oz) plain flour, sifted
2 teaspoons baking powder
Grated rind and juice of half a small orange
1 egg white, beaten
100g (4oz) caster sugar for dredging

Makes approximately 24 biscuits

Preheat the oven to 190°C, 375°F, gas mark 5. Grease two or three baking trays. Beat together the butter and sugar until light and fluffy. Add the egg yolk, flour, baking powder and orange rind and juice. Mix thoroughly to a stiff paste and knead until smooth. On a lightly floured board, roll out to a thickness of 0.5cm (¼in) and cut into rounds using a 6cm (2½in) cutter. Place on the prepared trays, leaving room for the biscuits to spread, brush the top of each with beaten egg white, dredge with caster sugar and bake for 10 minutes until pale golden. Remove from the oven and leave to cool for 5 minutes on the trays before lifting on to a wire rack to cool completely.

These biscuits are also excellent made with lemon juice and rind instead of orange.

Gypsy Creams

Some people define a gypsy cream as a chocolate or orange version of the Custard Cream but traditionally the recipe does not include either of those additional flavourings. The soft texture and creamy filling calls for a cup of Earl Grey with its citrus notes of bergamot, or a jasmine green from China.

FOR THE BISCUITS
175g (6oz) butter, softened
50g (2oz) white shortening (Trex or similar)
175g (6oz) caster sugar
2 teaspoons golden syrup
225g (8oz) plain wholemeal flour, sifted
1 teaspoon baking powder
1 teaspoon bicarbonate of soda

FOR THE FILLING
100g (4oz) butter, softened
50g (2oz) cream cheese
100g (4oz) icing sugar, sifted
50g (2oz) cocoa powder, sifted

Makes 24 double biscuits

Preheat the oven to 150°C, 300°F, gas mark 2. Grease two or three baking trays. Beat together the butter, white shortening and sugar until light and fluffy. Add the syrup and beat again. Add the flour, baking powder and bicarbonate of soda and mix thoroughly. On a lightly floured board, roll out and cut into rounds using a 5cm (2in) cutter. Place on the prepared trays, leaving plenty of room for the biscuits to spread, and bake for 20–25 minutes until firm and golden. Remove from the oven and lift on to a wire rack to cool. To make the filling, beat all the ingredients until light and fluffy and use to sandwich the biscuits together.

Macaroons

Dating back to 18th-century France, macaroons are a very traditional but also very modern mixture of egg whites, ground almonds and sugar. All the smartest tea places now serve tiny double-layer macaroons in different flavours and colours including rose, pistachio, matcha green tea, violet and fig, mango, raspberry and chocolate.

2 egg whites
100g (4oz) ground almonds
200g (7oz) caster sugar
25g (1oz) granulated sugar
15g (½oz) rice flour
1 teaspoon almond essence
Whole or split blanched almonds to decorate

Makes 18–20 macaroons

Preheat the oven to 180°C, 350°F, gas mark 4. Cover three baking trays with sheets of rice paper or non-stick greaseproof paper. Beat the egg whites for 3–4 minutes with an electric beater. Leave to rest for 4–5 minutes, then beat again until thick and white. Fold in the remaining ingredients and place the mixture in a piping bag fitted with a plain 1cm (½in) nozzle. Pipe small circles of the mixture on to the paper, leaving room for the macaroons to spread. Place a whole or split almond in the middle of each and bake for 10–15 minutes until pale golden. Remove from the oven and leave to cool on the trays. If using rice paper, cut round each macaroon. If using non-stick greaseproof paper, the macaroons should lift off easily.

Wholemeal Shortbread

Shortbreads date back to Roman times when the soft buttery cake was shared by bride and groom at their wedding ceremony to mark the beginning of a successful marriage. In later times, it evolved into a crumbly cake that was broken over the heads of the newly united couple as they stepped over the threshold of their new home to bring wealth, health and happiness.

150g (5oz) plain wholemeal flour
150g (5oz) plain white flour, sifted
150g (5oz) ground semolina
150g (5oz) demerara sugar

275g (10oz) slightly salted
   butter, softened
A little demerara sugar for
   sprinkling on top

Makes 16 fingers

Preheat the oven to 150°C, 300°F, gas mark 2. Grease a 17.5 x 27.5cm (7 x 11in) Swiss roll tin. Mix together the dry ingredients. Cut the butter into small pieces and rub into the flour with the fingertips. Work the mixture together to form a soft dough. Press into the prepared tin, smooth the top and prick all over with a fork. Bake for 1 hour 20 minutes until pale golden. Remove from the oven and sprinkle the demerara sugar over the top. Leave to cool in the tin for about 10 minutes. Using a sharp knife, cut into fingers and leave in the tin to finish cooling.

Date and Cinnamon Shortbread

350g (12oz) plain flour, sifted
1½ teaspoons ground cinnamon
250g (9oz) butter, softened
175g (6oz) light soft brown sugar
175g (6oz) stoned dates, chopped small

Makes 16 fingers

Preheat the oven to 180°C, 350°F, gas mark 4. Grease a 17.5 x 27.5cm (7 x 11in) Swiss roll tin. Mix together the flour and cinnamon and rub in the butter. Add the sugar and dates and stir well. Turn into the prepared tin and press down, smoothing the top with a palette knife. Bake for 30 minutes until golden. Remove from the oven and leave to cool in the tin. When cold, cut into fingers and lift carefully from the tin.

Cakes

Scones, muffins and fruited buns can be bought in supermarkets but teatime cakes really are more exciting and satisfying when they are homemade. Thrill family and friends with scrummy chocolate cakes, fruit cakes packed full of tea-plumped vine fruits or locally-grown apples and plums, or subtly flavoured with honey, saffron, spices, slivers of dried apricots and the wonderful texture of hazelnuts and almonds. Teatime wouldn't be teatime without such treats!

Sunday-best Chocolate Cake

A sumptuous cake for special occasions, the ingredients include two sorts of chocolate – cocoa powder and white chocolate. Cocoa powder is made by grinding down the seeds found inside cocoa pods into a thick creamy paste and then separating the cocoa butter from the cocoa solids. The cocoa solids can be dried into cocoa powder and the cocoa butter is used as the base for rich, smooth, creamy white chocolate.

FOR THE CAKE
225g (8oz) plain wholemeal flour, sifted
5 level teaspoons baking powder
225g (8oz) butter, softened
225g (8oz) light or dark soft brown sugar
5 large eggs, beaten
3 tablespoons cocoa powder, sifted

FOR THE FILLING AND TOPPING
350ml (12fl oz) single cream
675g (24oz) white chocolate, grated
Grated dark chocolate, curls of white chocolate
   or chocolate buttons, to decorate

Makes 1 x 20cm (8in) 3-tier cake

Preheat the oven to 160°C, 325°F, gas mark 3. Grease and line three 20cm (8in) round sandwich tins. Place all the ingredients for the cake in a large bowl and beat thoroughly to give a soft, dropping consistency (add a little water if too dry). Divide equally between the prepared tins and smooth the tops. Bake for about 30 minutes until the sponge springs back when lightly pressed. Remove from the oven and turn out on to a wire rack to cool. Next make the filling and topping. Bring the cream just to boiling point in a heavy pan and stir in the chocolate. Remove from the heat and stir until well blended. Leave in a cool place until it has achieved the right consistency for spreading. Use to sandwich the cakes together and to cover the top.

   Decorate with grated dark chocolate, fat curls of white chocolate or chocolate buttons. This makes a spectacular gateau, which is suitable for birthday parties or as a dinner-party dessert.

Chocolate Rum Cake

The flavours of chocolate and rum combine well together and this cake is a good example. Tea has a connection with rum since both were at one time smuggled into Britain together. Tea was so expensive and so heavily taxed that tea lovers found it difficult to afford a regular supply. So to provide cheaper tea, smugglers brought chests of tea (and bottles of rum, brandy, wines, perfume and other valuable items) from France and Holland where taxes were lower and they distributed the goods through a very active and successful local black market.

FOR THE CAKE
250g (9oz) butter, softened
250g (9oz) caster sugar
4 eggs
250g (9oz) self-raising flour, sifted
100g (4oz) drinking chocolate powder
40g (1½oz) cocoa powder, sifted
A few drops of vanilla essence
2–3 tablespoons dark rum
150ml (5fl oz) milk

FOR THE FILLING AND ICING
500g (18oz) icing sugar, sifted
40g (1½oz) cocoa powder, sifted
225g (8oz) butter, softened
175g (6oz) caster sugar
2 tablespoons dark rum
65ml (2½fl oz) milk

Makes 1 x 20cm (8in) round cake

Preheat the oven to 150°C, 300°F, gas mark 2. Grease and line a 20cm (8in) round tin. Beat together the butter and sugar until light and fluffy. Beat in the eggs, one at a time, beating hard after each addition. Combine the flour, drinking chocolate and cocoa and add to the mixture. Mix in carefully, taking care not to beat in any more air or the cake will flood over the top of the tin during cooking. Add the vanilla essence, rum and enough milk to mix to a soft, dropping consistency. Turn into the prepared tin, smooth the top and hollow out the middle a little. Bake for 1½–1¾ hours until a skewer comes out clean. Remove from the oven and allow to cool in the tin for about 15 minutes before turning on to a wire rack to cool completely.

To make the icing and filling, beat all the ingredients together until light and fluffy. Cut the cake horizontally through the middle. Spread half the mixture on to the base and sandwich the other half of the cake on top. Spread the remaining filling on top of the cake and decorate with grated chocolate, half walnuts or by making a pattern with the prongs of a fork. This is an impressive, deep cake that looks and tastes delicious.

Carob Crunch

For anyone who cannot eat chocolate, carob is an ideal alternative and is generally available in health-food shops. This recipe comes from Cliveden, an Italianate palace standing high above the River Thames in Berkshire. In the grounds is a small octagonal temple which serves as a tea house from where stunning views of the river and surrounding countryside may be enjoyed. On large estates like this, a whole day was sometimes set aside for an excursion to one or more of the follies, temples, pavilions and grottoes in the grounds. The assembly made their way on foot or by horse and carriage to the appointed rendezvous, indulged in a leisurely lunch or afternoon tea and then returned to the house.

225g (8oz) butter
25g (1oz) carob powder
225g (8oz) plain wholemeal flour, sifted
150g (5oz) light or dark soft brown sugar
100g (4oz) shredded coconut

Makes 12 pieces

Preheat the oven to 190°C, 375°F, gas mark 5. Grease a 17.5 x 27.5cm (7 x 11in) Swiss roll tin. In a medium-sized pan, melt the butter and add the carob powder. Stir over a gentle heat until the carob is dissolved. Add the flour, sugar and coconut and mix well. Turn into the prepared tin and press well down. Smooth the top and bake for 20–25 minutes until firm. Remove from the oven and leave to cool in the tin. When cold, cut into pieces and lift from the tin.

Plum Loaf

Unusually, this cake uses fresh plums that give a slightly tart flavour and juicy texture to the dough. Plums appear to have been grown in England since the 15th century and traditional plum-growing areas are in the vale of Evesham in Worcestershire, parts of Warwickshire and East Anglia. In Cornwall, the bitter-flavoured Kea plum grows on the Fal estuary.

225g (8oz) fresh plums, stoned (weighed after stoning)
100g (4oz) butter, softened
50g (2oz) light soft brown sugar
2 tablespoons golden syrup
2 eggs
225g (8oz) self-raising flour, sifted
2 teaspoons mixed spice
A little milk
Caster sugar for dusting

Makes 1 x 900g (2lb) loaf

Preheat the oven to 180°C, 350°F, gas mark 4. Grease and line a 900g (2lb) loaf tin. Chop the plums coarsely. Beat together the butter, sugar and syrup until light and fluffy. Add the eggs one at a time with a little flour, beating hard after each addition. Fold in the remaining flour, the spice and plums and enough milk to mix to a soft, dropping consistency. Turn into the prepared tin and bake for 1¼ hours until a skewer comes out clean. Remove from the oven and turn out on to a wire rack to cool. Before serving, dust with caster sugar.

This is an unusual cake and an excellent way to use spare fresh plums. The fruit gives the loaf a soft, moist texture and the spicy flavour complements the taste of the plums. Eat freshly baked, as the cake tends to dry out if left.

Kentish Hop Pickers' Cake

In the 17th and 18th centuries, up to 80,000 itinerant harvest workers arrived in Kent each September to gather the hops for beer making. Whole families would travel down from the East End of London and needed feeding by the hop farmers and this modern recipe developed from the cakes baked by the farmers' wives for teatime in the hop gardens.

275g (10oz) self-raising flour, sifted
1 teaspoon ground ginger
1 teaspoon mixed spice
175g (6oz) butter, softened
100g (4oz) light soft brown sugar
100g (4oz) sultanas
100g (4oz) currants
50g (2oz) mixed candied peel
400ml (15fl oz) milk
1 tablespoon black treacle
½ teaspoon bicarbonate of soda
1 teaspoon cream of tartar

Makes 1 x 900g (2lb) loaf

Preheat the oven to 160°C, 325°F, gas mark 3. Grease and line a 900g (2lb) loaf tin. Mix together the flour, ginger and spice and rub in the butter. Add the sugar and dried fruit and mix well. Warm the milk and treacle together and add the bicarbonate of soda and cream of tartar. Gradually add to the flour mixture and beat well. Pour into the prepared tin and bake for 1½ hours until a skewer comes out clean. Remove from the oven and turn out on to a wire rack to cool.

Simnel Cake

Simnel cakes were originally made for Mothering Sunday, the fourth Sunday in Lent, when children working away from home would return to their families in order to worship at the mother church. They would bring a cake as a gift for their mother, often made by their employer's wife. The eleven balls of marzipan represent the eleven apostles without Judas.

550g (1lb 4oz) marzipan

175g (6oz) butter, softened

150g (5oz) light soft brown sugar

3 eggs, beaten

15g (½oz) glycerine

15g (½oz) glucose

100g (4oz) strong plain white flour

50g (2oz) ordinary plain white flour

25g (1oz) ground almonds

1 teaspoon mixed spice

½ teaspoon grated nutmeg

350g (12oz) sultanas

250g (9oz) currants

100g (4oz) mixed candied peel

A little apricot jam for fixing the
  marzipan topping in place

Makes 1 x 8in (20cm) round cake

Preheat the oven to 180°C, 350°F, gas mark 4. Grease a 20cm (8in) round tin, line with a double layer of greaseproof paper and grease well. Divide the marzipan into three portions, one slightly smaller than the other two. Set the smallest portion aside and, on a sugared board, roll out one of the two equal portions to a circle just smaller than the diameter of the tin. Beat together the butter and sugar until light and fluffy. Add the beaten eggs, glycerine and glucose and beat again. Mix together the flour, almonds and spices and gradually add to the mixture, stirring gently to blend. Do not beat. Add the dried fruit and fold gently in. Turn half the mixture into the prepared tin and smooth the top. Place the circle of marzipan on top and then cover with the remaining cake mixture. Smooth the top and bake for 1 hour (if the top starts to become too brown, cover with a double layer of greaseproof paper), then reduce the oven temperature to 160°C, 325°F, gas mark 3 and bake for a further 45 minutes to 1 hour until a skewer comes out clean. Remove from the oven and leave to cool in the tin for about 15 minutes before turning out on to a wire rack to cool completely. When cold, brush the top with apricot jam. Roll out the second portion of marzipan to make a circle to fit the top of the cake. Put it in place and press gently to make sure it is firmly fixed. Form the remaining marzipan into eleven small balls and arrange them around the rim of the cake, sticking them on with a little apricot jam. Turn the grill to a moderate heat and place the cake underneath for a few minutes until the marzipan just begins to brown. To serve, wrap a wide yellow satin ribbon around the cake and fix with a pin. Arrange a small posy of fresh spring flowers on the top.

Chocolate Orange Drizzle Cake

Chocolate cakes are wonderful accompanied by a strong, black tea such as Kenya or a strong Ceylon or Assam. Brew the tea for 4–5 minutes to make sure that all the flavour and goodness are drawn out into the boiling water. Stronger teas often drink well with a little milk so add a small quantity of semi-skimmed, which works best in tea.

FOR THE CAKE
175g (6oz) butter, softened
175g (6oz) caster sugar
3 large eggs
Grated rind of 2 oranges
175g (6oz) self-raising flour, sifted
2 tablespoons milk

FOR THE TOPPING
the juice of 2 oranges
100g (4oz) granulated sugar
50g (2oz) milk or plain chocolate

Makes 1 x 900g (2lb) loaf or 17.5cm (7in) round cake

Preheat the oven to 180°C, 350°F, gas mark 4. Grease and line a 900g (2lb) loaf tin or a 17.5cm (7in) round tin. Cream together the butter and sugar until light and fluffy. Add the eggs, one at a time, and beat well. Add the grated orange rind, flour and milk and fold in with a metal spoon. Turn into the prepared tin, smooth the top and bake for 30–40 minutes until a skewer comes out clean. Remove from the oven and leave to cool in the tin. When cool, score the top of the cake lightly with a sharp knife. Put the orange juice and granulated sugar into a pan and heat gently until the sugar has dissolved. Bring to the boil and boil for 1–2 minutes. Pour over the cake. When all the juice has soaked in, carefully remove the cake from the tin. Melt the chocolate and pour over the top. Make a pattern with the prongs of a fork and leave to set.

Right: Chocolate Orange Drizzle Cake
Next page: Simnel Cake

Banana and Fruit Cake

This Irish recipe from Rowallane in County Down is excellent with a cup of Earl Grey. The recipe for blending bergamot with black China tea to make this very popular flavoured tea is said to have been given to a British diplomat in gratitude when he saved a mandarin's life while on a visit to China. It is said that when the diplomat returned to England, he presented it to the then Prime Minister, Earl Grey, who had the tea blended by his tea merchant and drank it as his favourite blend.

75g (3oz) butter, softened
100g (4oz) light or dark soft brown sugar
3 tablespoons clear honey
2 eggs, beaten
2 ripe bananas, mashed
225g (8oz) self-raising flour
1 teaspoon allspice
¼ teaspoon bicarbonate of soda
¼ teaspoon salt
225g (8oz) raisins

Makes 1 x 900g (2lb) loaf

Preheat the oven to 180°C, 350°F, gas mark 4. Grease and line a 900g (2lb) loaf tin. Beat together the butter and sugar until light and fluffy. Add the honey, eggs and bananas and beat well. Mix together the flour, allspice, bicarbonate of soda, salt and raisins and fold into the banana mixture. Mix well and then turn into the prepared tin. Bake for 1–1¼ hours until a skewer comes out clean. Remove from the oven and turn out on to a wire rack to cool.

Left: Banana and Fruit Cake
Previous page: Cornish Black Cake

Cornish Black Cake

Typical of recipes from this part of England, Cornish Black Cake uses several different spices and plenty of dried fruits, all of which would, in the past, have been brought into the country through the Cornish ports. Some recipes include dark molasses sugar to give an even richer colour to the mixture.

175g (6oz) butter, softened
175g (6oz) caster sugar
3–4 eggs, beaten
100g (4oz) plain flour, sifted
100g (4oz) ground rice
½ teaspoon mixed spice
¼ teaspoon grated nutmeg
½ teaspoon ground cinnamon
½ teaspoon baking powder
½ teaspoon bicarbonate of soda
450g (1lb) currants
100g (4oz) mixed candied peel
50g (2oz) sultanas
50g (2oz) raisins
75g (3oz) almonds, blanched and chopped
1 tablespoon brandy
A little milk for mixing

Makes 1 x 20cm (8in) round cake

Preheat the oven to 170°C, 325°F, gas mark 3. Grease and line a 20cm (8in) round tin. Beat together the butter and sugar until light and fluffy. Add the eggs, flour, ground rice, spices, baking powder, bicarbonate of soda, dried fruit, almonds and brandy and mix carefully until all the ingredients are evenly distributed. If necessary add a little milk to give a soft mixture. Turn into the prepared tin, smooth the top and bake for 1 hour. Reduce the oven temperature to 140°C, 275°F, gas mark 1 and cook for a further 1–1½ hours until a skewer comes out clean. Remove from the oven and leave to cool in the tin for 15 minutes, then turn out on to a wire rack to cool completely.

Old Peculier Fruit Cake

Old Peculier beer is brewed by Theakstons, founded in Yorkshire in 1827. Its rich, dark, smooth character adds the subtle, sweet flavour of hops to this fruit cake.

100g (4oz) butter, softened
50g (2oz) light soft brown sugar
50g (2oz) caster sugar
2 eggs
75g (3oz) plain flour, sifted
75g (3oz) self-raising flour, sifted
100g (4oz) currants
50g (2oz) raisins
50g (2oz) sultanas
Juice and grated rind of 1 lemon
70ml (2¾fl oz) Theakston's Old Peculier ale

Makes 1 x 900g (2lb) loaf

Grease and line a 900g (2lb) loaf tin. Beat together the butter and sugar until light and fluffy. Add the eggs one at a time and beat well. Fold in the flour, dried fruit and lemon juice and rind. Add the Old Peculier and stir well. Turn into the prepared tin, cover and leave to stand overnight. The next day preheat the oven to 150°C, 300°F, gas mark 2. Bake the cake for 1¾–2 hours until a skewer comes out clean. Remove from the oven and turn out on to a wire rack to cool.

The addition of the Theakston's Old Peculier strong Yorkshire ale is what makes this cake so distinctive.

Boiled Whiskey Cake

For festive occasions, the Irish added all the usual spices, butter and dried fruits to their plainer, everyday bread and cake mixtures to make them a little more special, and they also included one more, very Irish ingredient – whiskey! This recipe comes from Castle Ward in County Down where the wife of the 6th Viscount Bangor made a habit of serving afternoon tea to a number of guests in her sitting room. She used a willow-pattern tea service whose decoration is based on a Chinese tale of love and family intrigue.

275g (10oz) raisins and currants
225ml (8fl oz) water
225g (8oz) light or dark soft brown sugar
100g (4oz) butter
225g (8oz) plain flour, sifted
2 teaspoons mixed spice
1½ teaspoons bicarbonate of soda
1½ teaspoons ground ginger
2 large eggs, beaten
50ml (2fl oz) Irish whiskey

Makes 1 x 900g (2lb) loaf

Preheat the oven to 160°C, 325°F, gas mark 3. Grease and line a 900g (2lb) loaf tin. Put the mixed fruit, water, sugar and butter into a pan and bring to the boil, stirring occasionally. Leave to cool for a few minutes. Add a little of the flour, the mixed spice, bicarbonate of soda and ginger, then mix and leave to stand until cool. Add the beaten eggs, the whiskey and the remaining flour, mix well and turn into the prepared tin. Bake for 1½–1¾ hours until a skewer comes out clean. Remove from the oven and turn out on to a wire rack to cool.

Giant's Boiled Fruit Cake

The Irish drink more tea than any other nation in the world, Britain and the Arab states coming next in the list of great tea consumers. The strong black tea that they like to drink with milk and sugar is excellent with a slice of this fruit cake from Giant's Causeway.

175g (6oz) butter, softened
175g (6oz) granulated or caster sugar
300ml (10fl oz) water
100g (4oz) raisins
100g (4oz) sultanas
100g (4oz) currants
50g (2oz) glacé cherries, halved
225g (8oz) plain flour, sifted
2 teaspoons mixed spice
1 teaspoon baking powder
1 teaspoon ground ginger
50g (2oz) walnuts, roughly chopped
2 large eggs, beaten

Makes 1 x 900g (2lb) loaf

Put the butter, sugar, water, dried fruit and glacé cherries into a pan. Bring to the boil and simmer for 10 minutes. Remove from the heat and leave to stand overnight. The next day preheat the oven to 180°C, 350°F, gas mark 4. Grease and line a 900g (2lb) loaf tin. Mix together the dry ingredients and walnuts and add to the boiled mixture with the beaten eggs. Mix thoroughly and turn into the prepared tin. Bake for 1–1½ hours until a skewer comes out clean. Remove from the oven and leave to cool in the tin for about 15 minutes before turning out on to a wire rack to cool completely.

Wholemeal Cider Cake

Devonshire apples have been used to make cider since the 13th century and in the 17th century the orchards were extended with the sole purpose of manufacturing more cider. Use some to soak dried fruit before mixing into a fruit cake and it adds an extra zing to the final flavour.

100g (4oz) sultanas
75g (3oz) currants
25g (1oz) mixed candied peel
150ml (5fl oz) cider
150g (5oz) self-raising wholemeal flour, sifted
75g (3oz) dark soft brown sugar
50g (2oz) hazelnuts or blanched almonds, chopped
Finely grated rind of 1 lemon
Finely grated rind of 1 orange
1 eating apple, peeled, cored and chopped
2 medium eggs, beaten

Makes 1 x 900g (2lb) loaf

Put the dried fruit and the cider into a pan and bring to the boil. Remove from the heat and leave to stand overnight. The following day preheat the oven to 180°C, 350°F, gas mark 4. Grease and line a 900g (2lb) loaf tin. Mix together the flour, sugar, nuts, orange and lemon rind, apple and beaten eggs and pour in the cider mixture. Beat thoroughly, then turn into the prepared tin. Bake for about 1 hour until a skewer comes out clean. Remove from the oven and turn out on to a wire rack to cool.

Traditional Christmas Cake

FOR THE CAKE
225g (8oz) currants
225g (8oz) sultanas
225g (8oz) raisins
100g (4oz) glacé cherries, chopped
¼ glass brandy and port, mixed
1 teaspoon vanilla essence
1 teaspoon almond essence
225g (8oz) butter, softened
225g (8oz) soft brown sugar
4 large eggs, separated
225g (8oz) self-raising flour, sifted
1 teaspoon baking powder
1 teaspoon mixed spice

FOR THE DECORATION
225g (8oz) apricot jam
2–3 tablespoons water
550g (1¼lb) marzipan

FOR THE ICING
3 egg whites
675g (1½lb) icing sugar, sifted
1 tablespoon lemon juice
1 teaspoon glycerine

Makes 1 x 20cm (8in) square cake or 1 x 22.5cm (9in) round cake

Place the dried fruit, cherries, brandy and port, vanilla essence and almond essence in a bowl and leave to soak overnight. The next day preheat the oven to 150°C, 300°F, gas mark 2. Grease and line a 20cm (8in) square tin or a 22.5cm (9in) round tin. Beat together the butter and sugar. Beat the egg yolks and add with the fruit mixture to the fat and sugar, mixing well. Mix together the flour, baking powder and spice and add to the mixture. Stir thoroughly. Beat the egg whites until stiff and stir in. Turn into the prepared tin and bake for 2–2½ hours until a skewer comes out clean. Remove from the oven and leave in the tin for 30 minutes before turning out on to a wire rack to cool.

To decorate, heat the apricot jam and water in a small pan until the jam is dissolved. Push through a sieve and place in a clean pan. Bring back to the boil and simmer until fairly thick and smooth. Brush the mixture on to the outside of the cake. On a sugared surface, roll out two-thirds of the marzipan to form a rectangle as wide as the depth of the cake and twice as long. Place around the sides of the cake and press the ends well together. Roll out the remaining marzipan to make a circle to fit the top of the cake and put in place. Press the edges well together ensuring that the joins are neat. Leave in a warm room for 5–6 days until the marzipan has dried.

To make the icing, beat the egg whites until very frothy. Add half the icing sugar and beat in with a wooden spoon. Add the lemon juice, the glycerine and the remaining sugar and beat until the icing forms soft peaks. Cover with a damp cloth and leave in the bowl for a few hours to allow some of the air to escape. If the icing needs thickening, add a little more sugar as necessary.

Spice Cake

This is made to a recipe from Clandon Park in Surrey, a Georgian country house that has strong link to Catherine of Braganza, Portuguese princess who married Charles II in 1662 and is responsible for introducing tea to the English court. Portugal and Holland were the first European countries to start trading with China and brought home cargoes of tea, which were re-exported to other European cities including London. Catherine had grown up drinking tea and is said to have brought some with her when she sailed from Lisbon for her marriage.

450g (1lb) plain flour, sifted
4 teaspoons mixed spice
a pinch of salt
225g (8oz) Trex or similar white shortening, softened
175g (6oz) caster sugar
175g (6oz) sultanas
175g (6oz) currants
300ml (10fl oz) milk
2 teaspoons white wine vinegar
2 teaspoons bicarbonate of soda
2 tablespoons demerara sugar for sprinkling

Makes 1 x 20cm (8in) square cake

Preheat the oven to 160°C, 325°F, gas mark 3. Grease and line a 20cm (8in) square tin. Mix together the flour, spice and salt and rub in the fat. Add the caster sugar and dried fruit and mix well. Mix together the milk, vinegar and bicarbonate of soda and add to the mixture. Mix to a soft, fairly wet dough and turn into the prepared tin. Smooth the top and sprinkle with the demerara sugar. Bake for 1–1¼ hours until a skewer comes out clean. Remove from the oven and leave to cool in the tin.

Boodle Cake

The quirky name of this cake may come from Boodles Club that was founded in 1752 in St James's Street, London, and gave its name to a popular orange fool. Or it may derive from an old noun meaning a delight, dessert, feast, luxury, tidbit or treat! This recipe comes from Polesden Lacey where plenty of boodles were enjoyed at the afternoon teas hosted by Mrs Ronald Greville over the first few decades of the 20th century.

275g (10oz) butter, softened
450g (1lb) plain flour, sifted
275g (10oz) light soft brown or raw cane sugar
450g (1lb) raisins
2 eggs, beaten
300ml (10fl oz) milk

Makes 1 x 22.5cm (9in) square cake

Preheat the oven to 160°C, 325°F, gas mark 3. Grease and line a 22.5cm (9in) square tin. Rub the butter into the flour until the mixture resembles breadcrumbs. Stir in the sugar and raisins. Add the eggs and milk and mix to a soft dough. Turn into the prepared tin, spread evenly with a palette knife and bake for 2 hours until a skewer comes out clean. Remove from the oven and turn out on to a wire rack to cool.

Mincemeat Cake

Mincemeat really was once minced meat mixed up with spices, dried fruit, lemon peel, grated apple and brandy or rum. In most modern mincemeats, the only remaining part of the meat is suet, although vegetarian varieties replace this with butter. If eating a strongly spiced cake or pastry like this at teatime, choose a tea like China black Keemun or Yunnan, a Nilgiri from southern India or a strong English Breakfast blend.

225g (8oz) self-raising flour, sifted
150g (5oz) butter, softened
150g (5oz) light or dark soft brown sugar
75g (3oz) sultanas
450g (1lb) mincemeat
2 eggs, beaten
25–50g (1–2oz) flaked almonds

Makes 1 x 20cm (8in) round cake

Preheat the oven to 160°C, 325°F, gas mark 3. Grease and line a 20cm (8in) round tin. Keeping aside the flaked almonds, put all the ingredients into a bowl and mix thoroughly. Turn into the prepared tin and sprinkle the flaked almonds over the top. Bake for 1¾ hours until a skewer comes out clean. Remove from the oven and leave in the tin for about 15 minutes before turning out on to a wire rack to cool completely.

Orange Gingerbread

In Britain's past, gingerbreads and ginger biscuits were sold at medieval fairs and were often made in special shapes for different locations. In Hampshire, Gingerbread Husbands were popular, while in Bath, heart-shaped Gingerbread Valentines were sold. Some were soft cakes served in slices while others were crunchy biscuits. This orange version comes from Bateman's in Sussex where Rudyard Kipling perhaps took tea with a slice of gingerbread in the entrance hall – the favourite setting for afternoon tea.

100g (4oz) butter
100g (4oz) black treacle
100g (4oz) golden syrup
50g (2oz) light or dark soft brown sugar
1 teaspoon bicarbonate of soda
150ml (5fl oz) orange juice
225g (8oz) plain wholemeal flour, sifted
1 heaped teaspoon mixed spice
2 heaped teaspoons ground ginger
2 eggs, beaten
40g (1½oz) flaked almonds to decorate

Makes 12 pieces

Preheat the oven to 150°C, 300°F, gas mark 2. Grease and line a 17.5 x 27.5cm (7 x 11in) Swiss roll tin. In a medium-sized pan melt together the butter, treacle, syrup and sugar over a low heat. Dissolve the bicarbonate of soda in the orange juice and add to the mixture. Stir well. Add the flour, spice, ginger and beaten eggs and beat well to a smooth batter. Pour into the prepared tin and scatter the flaked almonds over the top. Bake for 1 hour until firm and well risen. Remove from the oven and leave to cool in the tin. When cold, cut into bars and lift carefully from the tin.

Grasmere Gingerbread

Grasmere Gingerbread is rather different from other gingerbreads. Instead of being a moist soft cake or a crunchy biscuit, it is almost like a shortbread and is crumbly and light. In the 19th century, it was given as a reward to the children who brought rushes to cover the unpaved floor of the local church of St Oswald.

275g (10oz) plain flour, sifted
1 teaspoon ground ginger
½ teaspoon ground cinnamon
Pinch of salt
100g (4oz) stoned dates, chopped
150g (5oz) black treacle
75g (3oz) butter
100g (4oz) dark soft brown sugar
1 egg, beaten
¾ teaspoon bicarbonate of soda
    dissolved in 3 tablespoons milk

Makes 16 pieces

Preheat the oven to 170°C, 325°F, gas mark 3. Grease and line a 25cm (10in) square tin. Mix together the flour, ginger, cinnamon and salt. Add the dates. Melt the treacle, butter and sugar together over a gentle heat, then leave to cool for a few minutes. Add the flour mixture and mix thoroughly. Add the beaten egg, bicarbonate of soda and milk and blend well to a fairly wet consistency, adding a little more milk if too dry. Turn into the prepared tin and bake for 1½ hours until a skewer comes out clean. Remove from the oven and turn out on to a wire rack to cool. When cold, cut into pieces.

Simone Sekers's Fruit Parkin

Parkin is gingerbread made with oatmeal instead of flour and has a lovely nutty texture. Parkins are traditionally a Hallowe'en speciality and probably derive from the pagan practice of baking oatmeal and spice cakes for celebrations marking the beginning of winter. In Lancashire, the cakes were called Har Cakes after god Har, and in Derbyshire, they were named after Thor, the Scandinavian god of thunder, war and agriculture. The cakes were sometimes referred to as 'tharve' cakes (the hearth cake) since they were cooked on a bakestone on an open kitchen fire.

400ml (15fl oz) water
100g (4oz) lard
175g (6oz) light or dark soft brown sugar
225g (8oz) golden syrup
225g (8oz) black treacle
100g (4oz) currants
50g (2oz) mixed candied peel
450g (1lb) plain flour, sifted
225g (8oz) medium oatmeal
2 teaspoons mixed spice
1½ teaspoons ground ginger
Pinch of salt and 1 teaspoon bicarbonate
    of soda dissolved in a little water

Makes 24 slices

Preheat the oven to 160°C, 325°F, gas mark 3. Grease and line a deep roasting tin measuring approximately 20 x 30cm (8 x 12in). Warm together the water, lard, sugar, syrup and treacle until melted. When cool, add all the other ingredients and mix thoroughly so that all are evenly distributed. Turn into the prepared tin and bake for 1–1½ hours until firm and well risen. Remove from the oven and leave to cool in the tin. When cold, cut into squares or slices.

Dolce Torinese

An easy and delicious cake or dessert, the almonds give a lovely nutty texture. They are rich in vitamins, fibre, magnesium and antioxidants. In fact they are thought to contain similar levels of antioxidants as broccoli and tea. And a slice of Dolce Torinese is much nicer with a cup of tea than with a plateful of broccoli!

100g (4oz) good-quality plain chocolate
1½ tablespoons sherry, brandy or rum
100g (4oz) unsalted butter, softened
150g (5oz) caster sugar
1 egg, separated
65g (2½oz) blanched almonds, shredded
6 butter biscuits, broken into small pieces
Icing sugar for dredging
Whipped cream (optional)

Makes 1 x 20cm (8in) round cake

Grease and line a 20cm (8in) round, loose-bottomed tin. Melt the chocolate and stir in the alcohol. Beat the butter, sugar and egg yolk until light and fluffy. Stir in the almonds and the chocolate mixture. Beat the egg white until very stiff and fold into the mixture. Add the broken biscuits and stir until evenly distributed. Turn into the prepared tin and smooth the top. Place the tin in the refrigerator and leave to set overnight. When ready to serve, turn out and dust with icing sugar. If liked, pipe whipped cream around the edge, or serve separately.

This rich cake makes an excellent dessert for a special dinner party.

Light Sponge Cake

This is a recipe from Chirk Castle in Wales where afternoon tea was a very elegant but small meal consisting of sandwiches the size of a postage stamp. Sometimes in cold weather a dish of hot buttered muffins or warm scones were also served. One footman who used to be responsible for taking tea into the salon once said, 'When clearing away the teas I always remember you had to eat at least four sandwiches to even taste them!'

200g (7oz) granulated or caster sugar
2 large or 3 medium eggs
150g (5oz) self-raising flour, sifted
a pinch of salt
1 teaspoon baking powder
100ml (4fl oz) milk
50g (2oz) butter
2–3 drops vanilla essence

Makes 1 x 20cm (8in) round cake

Preheat the oven to 160°C, 325°F, gas mark 3. Grease and line a 20cm (8in) round tin. Beat together the sugar and eggs until thick and creamy. Add the flour, salt and baking powder and mix well. Put the milk in a small pan and heat gently. Melt the butter in the milk and bring to the boil. When boiling, add to the flour mixture with the vanilla essence and beat well to give a runny consistency. Turn into the prepared tin and bang the tin sharply on the table to remove air bubbles. Bake for 20–25 minutes until a skewer comes out clean. Remove from the oven and cool in the tin for 15 minutes before turning out on to a wire rack to cool completely.

This cake is quick and easy to make, and is delicious served with fruit and cream. It is ideal for freezing.

Almond-topped Apricot Cake

This really delicious cake is made to a recipe from Petworth House in West Sussex which has an impressive collection of tea porcelain. The word 'china' entered the English language in the 17th century when porcelain first arrived from China. Dishes, plates, bowls and saucers were described as 'cheyney', 'chenea', 'chiney' or 'cheny' and, since the European potters only knew how to make tableware from earthernware or stoneware, these Oriental wares were much sought after.

FOR THE CAKE
175g (6oz) butter, softened
175g (6oz) caster sugar
3 eggs
175g (6oz) self-raising flour, sifted
75g (3oz) ground almonds
100g (4oz) ready-to-use dried apricots, chopped

FOR THE TOPPING
50g (2oz) butter
50g (2oz) demerara sugar
1 tablespoon golden syrup
50g (2oz) flaked almonds

Makes 1 x 22.5cm (9in) round cake

Preheat the oven to 180°C, 350°F, gas mark 4. Grease and base-line a 22.5cm (9in) loose-bottomed round tin. Beat together the butter and sugar until light and fluffy. Beat in the eggs one at a time, adding a tablespoon of flour with each. Fold in the remaining flour, the ground almonds and the apricots and mix well. Turn into the prepared tin and bake for 40 minutes. Meanwhile prepare the topping. In a small pan mix together the butter, sugar and syrup and heat gently until the sugar dissolves. Remove from the heat and stir in the almonds. When the 40 minutes' cooking time is up, remove the cake from the oven and spoon the topping over. Return to the oven and bake for a further 10–15 minutes until golden brown. Remove from the oven and leave to cool in the tin.

Right: Almond-topped Apricot Cake
Next page: Light Sponge Cake

Carrot Cake with Lime Topping

This is another indulgent cake that should be eaten with little pastry forks. These small, three-pronged tea forks developed from Victorian dessert forks in the second half of the 19th century. So that a little pressure could safely be exerted on a fruit tartlet or slice of Madeira cake, the first two narrow prongs of the fork were fused to make one wider prong that acted as a cutting edge. Like tea knives and silver teaspoons, the forks usually came in little boxes of six.

FOR THE CAKE

2 eggs

100g (4oz) light soft brown sugar

75ml (3fl oz) oil (sunflower, vegetable or corn)

100g (4oz) self-raising flour, sifted

175g (6oz) grated carrot

1 teaspoon ground cinnamon

50g (2oz) shredded coconut

FOR THE TOPPING

75g (3oz) cream cheese

75g (3oz) butter

50g (2oz) icing sugar

Grated rind of 1 lime

Toasted coconut and grated lime to decorate (optional)

Makes 1 x 900g (2lb) loaf or 1 x 17.5cm (7in) round cake

Preheat the oven to 190°C, 375°F, gas mark 5. Grease and line a 900g (2lb) loaf tin or a 17.5cm (7in) round tin. Beat together the eggs and sugar until very creamy. Add the oil and beat hard. Fold in the remaining ingredients and turn into the prepared tin. Smooth the top, then slightly hollow out the middle. Bake for 35–40 minutes until golden and well risen and a skewer comes out clean. Remove from the oven and turn out on to a wire rack to cool. To make the topping, beat the ingredients together until light and creamy and spread over the top of the cake. Make a pattern with the prongs of a fork.

Left: Carrot Cake with Lime Topping
Previous page: Kedleston Marmalade Cake

Kedleston Marmalade Cake

Marmalades started life as a sort of quince (marmelo) jam but, in the 17th century, were made in England with oranges instead. The bitter sweet flavour adds an interesting bite to this cake which goes very well with Ceylon or Assam tea.

175g (6oz) butter, softened
50g (2oz) light or dark soft brown sugar
4 tablespoons golden syrup
2 eggs
150g (5oz) orange marmalade
275g (10oz) self-raising wholemeal flour, sifted
2 teaspoons baking powder
½ teaspoon ground ginger
3–4 tablespoons orange juice

Makes 1 x 20cm (8in) round cake

Preheat the oven to 180°C, 350°F, gas mark 4. Grease and line a 20cm (8in) round tin. Beat together the butter and sugar until light and fluffy. Add the syrup and beat again. Whisk together the eggs and marmalade and add to the mixture with the flour, baking powder and ginger. Stir in the orange juice to give a soft, dropping consistency. Turn into the prepared tin and bake for about 1 hour until a skewer comes out clean. Remove from the oven and leave to cool in the tin for 15 minutes before turning out on to a wire rack to cool completely.

Carrot and Pineapple Cake

English recipes have included carrots in sweet dishes and cakes since medieval times but carrot cakes became particularly popular at teatime in the late 1960s. This one is made to a recipe from East Riddlesden Hall in West Yorkshire where the drawing room has on show a most unusual teapot in the form of a Chinese peach-shaped wine ewer. It is a 'Cadogan teapot' named after the Honorable Mrs Cadogan who brought it to England. It has no lid but fills from the bottom through a long internal tube that runs upwards into the pot and stops the tea from flowing out again.

225g (8oz) rice flour
200g (7oz) caster sugar
½ teaspoon salt
½ teaspoon bicarbonate of soda
100g (4oz) undrained crushed pineapple
200g (7oz) grated carrot
100ml (4fl oz) corn or vegetable oil
2 eggs, beaten
½ teaspoon vanilla essence
50g (2oz) walnuts, roughly chopped

Makes 1 x 900g (2lb) loaf

Preheat the oven to 190°C, 375°F, gas mark 5. Grease and line a 900g (2lb) loaf tin. Mix together the flour, sugar, salt and bicarbonate of soda. Add the pineapple, carrot, oil, eggs, vanilla essence and walnuts and mix thoroughly. Turn into the prepared tin and bake for 1–1½ hours until a skewer comes out clean. Remove from the oven and leave to cool in the tin for a few minutes before turning out on to a wire rack to cool completely.

American Zucchini Cake

Zucchini, or courgettes, are an unusual ingredient in a cake but like carrots, they make the dough soft and moist. This recipe is from Hidcote Manor Garden in Gloucestershire where it is said the National Trust first served teas to members of the public. The tea was brewed in the gardener's cottage and handed out through the window to thirsty visitors.

2 eggs
100ml (4fl oz) oil (corn, vegetable or sunflower)
225g (8oz) caster sugar
350g (12oz) grated courgettes
1½ teaspoons vanilla or almond essence
50g (2oz) chopped nuts or a mixture of 25g (1oz) chopped
    nuts and 25g (1oz) sultanas
175g (6oz) self-raising flour, sifted
1½ teaspoons ground cinnamon or mixed spice

Makes 1 x 900g (2lb) loaf

Preheat the oven to 160°C, 325°F, gas mark 3. Grease and line a 900g (2lb) loaf tin. Beat the eggs until light and foamy. Add the oil, sugar, courgettes and essence and mix lightly, until all the ingredients are evenly distributed. Fold in the nuts (or nuts and sultanas), flour and spice until well mixed and turn into the prepared tin. Bake for 1¼–1½ hours until a skewer comes out clean. Remove from the oven and turn out on to a wire rack to cool.

This is an excellent, unusual, moist cake.

Sticky Lemon Cake

This wonderfully tangy cake is made to a recipe from Castle Drogo in Devon which was built by Julius Drewe in 1900 to Sir Edwin Lutyens' design. Mr Drewe opened his own tea store (The Willow Pattern Tea Store) in 1878, then set up the Home and Colonial Stores in 1883 and sold so much tea that he became a millionaire. While he lived at Castle Drogo, tea was served each day in the library and was 'a wonderful meal with wafer-thin bread and butter, scones and jam and Devonshire cream – and cakes in great variety, followed by whatever fruit was in season'.

FOR THE CAKE
100g (4oz) butter, softened
100g (4oz) caster sugar
2 eggs
100g (4oz) self-raising flour, sifted
Grated rind and juice of half a lemon
1½ tablespoons icing sugar, sifted

FOR THE ICING
50–75g (2–3oz) icing sugar, sifted
Juice and finely grated rind of half a lemon

Makes 1 x 17.5cm (7in) round cake

Preheat the oven to 160°C, 325°F, gas mark 3. Grease and line a 17.5cm (7in) round tin. Beat together the butter and sugar until light and fluffy. Beat in the eggs, one at a time, whisking hard after the addition of each one. Fold in the flour and rind, mix well and turn into the prepared tin. Bake for 45 minutes until a skewer comes out clean. Remove from the oven and make several holes in the top of the cake with a skewer. Mix together the icing sugar and lemon juice and pour over the cake. Leave in the tin until absolutely cold. Meanwhile make the icing. Mix together the icing sugar, lemon rind and juice. When the cake is cold, turn out and ice with the prepared mixture.

Cornish Banana Cake

When afternoon tea is set out at home the various platters of sandwiches, scones and cakes are usually arranged on a table, trolley or sideboard. In tearooms and lounges, space-saving, three-tier, silver cake stands display the food and look spectacular with their neat finger sandwiches, warm scones and tiny French pastries. Dishes of jam and clotted cream are usually presented separately.

FOR THE CAKE
225g (8oz) very ripe bananas (weighed after peeling)
90g (3½oz) caster sugar
90g (3½oz) butter, softened
200g (7oz) self-raising flour, sifted
1 egg, beaten
½ teaspoon bicarbonate of soda
1 tablespoon milk
Whole, blanched almonds or slices of dried banana chips to decorate

FOR THE FILLING
1 ripe banana
50g (2oz) butter, softened
50g (2oz) caster sugar

FOR THE ICING
1 soft, very ripe banana
25g (1oz) cocoa powder, sifted
225g (8oz) icing sugar, sifted

Makes 1 x double layer 17.5cm (7in) round cake

Preheat the oven to 180°C, 350°F, gas mark 4. Grease two 17.5cm (7in) round sandwich tins. Mash the bananas and sugar together in a food processor or mixer. Beat in the butter, and add the flour and egg alternately. Dissolve the bicarbonate of soda in the milk and add to the mixture. Beat well to a fairly sticky batter. Turn into the prepared tins, smooth the tops and bake for 35–40 minutes until the sponge springs back when lightly pressed. Remove from the oven and turn on to a wire rack to cool. To make the filling, beat all the ingredients together until well mixed and use to sandwich the cakes together. For the icing, beat the ingredients together until dark and really smooth and spread on to the top of the cake. Decorate with the blanched almonds, walnut halves or dried banana chips.

Banana and Pineapple Cake

As the ritual of teatime developed through the second half of the 19th century, households acquired more and more porcelain teaware. In the early days of tea drinking in England, little tea bowls, saucers and dishes for sugar or bread and butter were not available as matching sets, but as afternoon tea became more and more popular the idea of the tea set gradually evolved and often included 12 tea cups or bowls, 12 coffee cups, 12 saucers, side plates, larger plates for bread and butter or cakes, teapots, milk jugs and sugar basins.

5 or 6 tinned pineapple rings
200g (7oz) plain flour, sifted
1 teaspoon ground cinnamon
½ teaspoon bicarbonate of soda
200g (7oz) caster sugar
100g (4oz) pecans or walnuts, roughly chopped
2 bananas, mashed
1 x 432g (15¼oz) can of crushed pineapple, drained
100ml (4fl oz) corn or sunflower oil
2 eggs

Makes 1 x 22.5cm (9in) ring cake

Preheat the oven to 180°C, 350°F, gas mark 4. Grease and line a 22.5cm (9in) ring tin and place the pineapple rings in the base of the tin. Mix together all the other ingredients and spoon into the tin. Bake for 30–35 minutes until a skewer comes out clean. Remove from the oven and leave to cool in the tin. When cold, turn out and peel off the greaseproof paper. Serve with the pineapple rings uppermost.

Orange and Lemon Cake

Invitations to afternoon tea were issued verbally or by a small card delivered one or two days before. No answer was required. On the subject of the correct time to arrive, one writer of etiquette books advised that 'the proper time is from four to seven'. Guests were not expected to stay throughout but to come and go as they pleased.

225g (8oz) butter, softened
225g (8oz) caster sugar
3 eggs
Juice and rind of half an orange
Juice and rind of half a lemon
225g (8oz) plain flour, sifted

Makes 1 x 20cm (8in) round cake

Preheat the oven to 160°C, 325°F, gas mark 3. Grease and line a 20cm (8in) round tin. Beat together the butter and sugar until light and fluffy. Add the eggs, orange and lemon rind and juice and beat well. Add the flour and beat carefully for a few seconds. Turn into the prepared tin and bake for 1 hour until a skewer comes out clean. Remove from the oven and leave to cool in the tin.

If liked, split in half and fill with butter filling made with the grated rind and juice from half a lemon and half an orange, 50g (2oz) softened butter and 175g (6oz) sifted icing sugar. Decorate the top by dredging with icing sugar or spread with glacé icing made by mixing together 175g (6oz) icing sugar and the juice and grated rind of half a lemon and half an orange.

Sussex Apple Cake

Sticky fingers from eating cakes like this demand elegant linen tea napkins. As early as 1773, inventories of household linens included such entries as '4 dozen Bird Eye Tea Napkens' (napkins made in two-colour, double-knit fabric). Victorian tea linens were often in white lace or linen decorated with drawn-thread work or embroidery, while the Edwardians seem to have preferred a cream-coloured background for their pretty tea sets.

225g (8oz) butter, softened

225g (8oz) dark soft brown sugar

3 large eggs

150g (5oz) walnuts, finely chopped or crushed

150g (5oz) sultanas or raisins

225g (8oz) wholemeal self-raising flour, sifted

400g (14oz) cooking apples, peeled, cored and grated

½ teaspoon ground cloves

Makes 1 x 22.5cm (9in) round cake

Preheat the oven to 180°C, 350°F, gas mark 4. Grease and base-line a 22.5cm (9in) loose-bottomed round tin. Beat together the butter and 175g (6oz) of the sugar until light and fluffy. Add the eggs and beat hard. Fold in 100g (4oz) of the walnuts, the sultanas or raisins and the flour, mixing well so that all the ingredients are evenly distributed. Put half the mixture into the prepared tin. Mix together the apples and cloves and spread over the layer of cake mixture. Spread the remaining cake mixture on top and smooth with a palette knife. Mix together the remaining sugar and walnuts and sprinkle evenly over the top of the cake. Bake for 1¼–1½ hours until the top is caramelized but not too brown. Remove from the oven and leave to cool in the tin.

Madeira Cake

This simple sponge cake was traditionally served with a glass of madeira wine but today it makes an excellent accompaniment to a cup of Ceylon or Darjeeling tea, or for a change, perhaps a China oolong or Keemun. It needs to be eaten very fresh when it is soft and light.

225g (8oz) plain flour, sifted
1 teaspoon baking powder
175g (6oz) butter, softened
175g (6oz) caster sugar
Grated rind of half a lemon
3 eggs
2 tablespoons milk

Makes 1 x 7in (17.5cm) round cake

Preheat the oven to 180°C, 350°F, gas mark 4. Grease and line a 17.5cm (7in) round tin. Mix together the flour and baking powder. Beat together the butter, sugar and lemon rind until light and fluffy. Beat in the eggs, one at a time, adding 2 tablespoons of flour with the last two. Fold in the remaining flour, then gently mix in the milk. Turn into the prepared tin and bake for 1 hour until a skewer comes out clean. Remove from the oven and turn out on to a wire rack to cool.

18th-Century Pepper Cake

Although generally used in savoury dishes, black pepper is sometimes added to cakes with ginger and other spices. Some recipes for this traditional Westmorland fruit cake also add dates and walnuts but this one from Wordsworth House in the Lake District uses cloves, currants, raisins and peel.

450g (1lb) plain flour, sifted
1 teaspoon baking powder
100g (4oz) butter, softened
225g (8oz) caster sugar
100g (4oz) currants
100g (4oz) raisins
25g (1oz) mixed candied peel
¼ teaspoon ground cloves
¼ teaspoon ground ginger
¼ teaspoon ground black pepper
225g (8oz) black treacle
2 eggs, beaten

Makes 1 x 22.5cm (9in) round cake

Preheat the oven to 150°C, 300°F, gas mark 2. Grease and line a 22.5cm (9in) round deep cake tin. Mix together the flour and baking powder and rub in the butter until the mixture resembles fine breadcrumbs. Add all the other ingredients and mix to a thick batter. Turn into the prepared tin and bake for 2–2½ hours until a skewer comes out clean. Remove from the oven and leave to cool in the tin for 15 minutes before turning out on to a wire rack to cool completely. When cool, wrap in foil or cling film and store for a few days before using.

The cake may be coated with marzipan and iced with a plain white icing made with 175–225g (6–8oz) icing sugar, sifted and mixed with 1–2 tablespoons cold water or lemon juice.

17th-Century Honey Cake

It is thought that a daily dose of honey helps to boost the body's supply of beneficial antioxidants that protect us against age-related diseases. Tea is also a source of antioxidants and offers protection against certain cancers and heart disease. So a slice of this honey cake with two or three cups of tea will not just taste good – it will do you good as well.

FOR THE CAKE
175g (6oz) butter, softened
175g (6oz) caster sugar
3 eggs, beaten
175g (6oz) white or wholemeal self-raising four, sifted
1 teaspoon baking powder
1 tablespoon clear honey
A few drops of almond essence

FOR THE TOPPING
1 dessertspoon clear honey
Juice of 1 lemon

FOR THE ICING
150g (5oz) cream cheese
Juice of half a lemon
175g (6oz) icing sugar, sifted

Makes 1 x 900g (2lb) loaf or 17.5cm (7in) round cake

Preheat the oven to 180°C, 350°F, gas mark 4. Grease and line a 900g (2lb) loaf tin or a 17.5cm (7in) round tin. Beat together the butter and sugar until light and fluffy. Add the eggs, flour and baking powder and beat hard. Add the honey and almond essence and continue beating for 1–2 minutes. Turn into the prepared tin and bake for 1–1¼ hours until a skewer comes out clean. (After half an hour, cover the top with a double layer of greaseproof paper as the cake tends to darken quite quickly.) Remove from the oven. Mix together the honey and lemon juice and pour over the top. Leave to cool in the tin, then turn out. Beat together the cream cheese, lemon juice and icing sugar and spread over the cooled cake. Make a pattern with the prongs of a fork and serve.

Streusal Crunchy Cake

Using muesli as one of the ingredients, this spiced, nutty cake has a wonderful texture and layers of interesting flavours. Muesli is generally considered to be a healthy food because it contains oats which help to reduce blood cholesterol, and nuts which are rich in omega-3 fatty acids and are good for the nervous system.

FOR THE CAKE
150g (5oz) self-raising flour, sifted
150g (5oz) light soft brown sugar
175g (6oz) butter, softened
3 eggs, beaten

FOR THE FILLING AND TOPPING
2 tablespoons muesli cereal
1 tablespoon light soft brown sugar
1 teaspoon ground cinnamon
50g (2oz) walnuts, roughly chopped

Makes 1 x 17.5cm (7in) round cake

Preheat the oven to 180°C, 350°F, gas mark 4. Grease and line a 17.5cm (7in) loose-bottomed round tin. Place the flour, sugar, butter and eggs together in a bowl and beat for 2 minutes. Turn half the mixture into the prepared tin and press down. Mix together the ingredients for the filling and topping and sprinkle two-thirds over the cake. Spread the remaining cake mixture on top and smooth. Sprinkle the remaining muesli mixture over the top and bake for 20–25 minutes until firm and browned. Remove from the oven and leave to cool in the tin.

Dorothy Wordsworth's Favourite Cake

Caraway seed is the fruit of a herb related to the parsley family and since medieval times has been used in breads, cakes and cheeses. Seed cakes were very popular in Victorian times when cookery books always included at least one recipe. The seed is thought to aid digestion.

175g (6oz) butter, softened
175g (6oz) caster sugar
3 eggs
3 teaspoons caraway seeds
225g (8oz) plain flour, sifted
1 teaspoon baking powder
Pinch of salt
1 tablespoon ground almonds
1 tablespoon milk

Makes 1 x 900g (2lb) loaf

Preheat the oven to 180°C, 350°F, gas mark 4. Grease and line a 900g (2lb) loaf tin. Beat together the butter and sugar until light and fluffy, then beat in the eggs. Add the caraway seeds, flour, baking powder, salt, almonds and milk and mix carefully so that all the ingredients are evenly distributed. Turn into the prepared tin and bake for 45–55 minutes until a skewer comes out clean. Remove from the oven and leave to cool in the tin.

Featherlight Wholewheat Cake

Using the correct measures when baking is obviously very important and it is equally important to use the correct measure when brewing tea. The best guideline is to allow 2.5–3g to 200ml of water. Different teas brew at different rates so use a timer to be sure not to spoil the tea. Small-leafed tea takes approximately 2–3 minutes to brew. Large-leafed tea needs 4–5 minutes.

FOR THE CAKE
100g (4oz) butter, softened
100g (4oz) light or dark soft brown sugar
2 egg yolks
1 tablespoon cold water
100g (4oz) wholewheat self-raising flour, sifted
2 egg whites

FOR THE FILLING AND ICING
200g (7oz) low-fat cream cheese
50g (2oz) icing sugar, sifted
75g (3oz) walnuts, chopped

TO DECORATE
9 half walnuts

Makes 1 x 17.5cm (7in) round cake

Preheat the oven to 180°C, 350°F, gas mark 4. Grease two 17.5cm (7in) round sandwich tins. Beat together the butter and sugar until light and fluffy. Beat together the egg yolks and water, add to the mixture and beat hard. Fold in the flour. Whisk the egg whites until stiff, then fold in. Turn into the prepared tins and smooth. Bake for 20–25 minutes until well risen and golden. Remove from the oven and leave to cool in the tins for 5 minutes, then turn out on to a wire rack to cool completely. Meanwhile beat together the ingredients for the filling until light and fluffy. When the cake is cold, spread half of the mixture on one cake and place the other cake on top. Ice with the remaining mixture and decorate with half walnuts.

Canons Ashby Coconut Cake

Canons Ashby in Northamptonshire was once famous for its local postman who doubled as hedge-clipper. One day when the owner, Sir Henry Dryden, was having a tea party on the lawn with his friends, he asked the postman to clip the yew trees while he was on the premises. As the guests watched him clip away, they decided to ask him to exercise his skills and give them each a haircut and, having preformed the task to their satisfaction, he joined the tea party!

FOR THE CAKE
100g (4oz) butter, softened
75g (3oz) light soft brown sugar
2 teaspoons almond essence
Grated rind of 1 lemon
1 egg, beaten
250g (9oz) plain flour, sifted
5-6 tablespoons plum jam

FOR THE TOPPING
1 egg, beaten
75g (3oz) light soft brown sugar
100g (4oz) shredded coconut

FOR DIPPING
175-225g (6-8oz) milk or plain chocolate

Makes 12 fingers

Preheat the oven to 180°C, 350°F, gas mark 4. Grease a 17.5 x 27.5cm (7 x 11in) Swiss roll tin. Beat together the butter, sugar, almond essence, lemon rind and egg. Add the flour and mix well. Press into the prepared tin and spread a layer of jam on top. Mix together the ingredients for the topping and spread over the jam. Bake for 20–30 minutes until firm and pale golden. Remove from the oven and leave to cool in the tin. When cold, cut into fingers and lift carefully from the tin. Melt the chocolate and dip both ends of each finger into it. Place carefully on a wire rack to set.

Pineapple Upside-Down Cake

A modern recipe served in the tearoom at Montacute House, an early 17th-century home whose 1728 inventory recorded two tea tables in the library. Tea tables started to appear in England in the 1680s and 90s, mostly purchased from Indonesia and Japan. In fact, so many foreign tea tables were imported that London cabinet-makers feared for their jobs and signed a petition against the practice.

175g (6oz) golden syrup
225g (8oz) tinned pineapple slices, drained
100g (4oz) butter, softened
100g (4oz) caster sugar
2 eggs, beaten
100g (4oz) self-raising flour, sifted
Pinch of salt
Pinch of ground cinnamon

Makes 1 x 15cm (6in) round cake

Preheat the oven to 160°C, 325°F, gas mark 3. Grease and line a 15cm (6in) round tin. Spread the syrup in the base of the tin and arrange the pineapple slices over the top. Beat together the butter and sugar until light and fluffy. Beat in the eggs, one at a time, adding 1 tablespoon of flour with each. Beat hard, then fold in the remaining flour with the salt and cinnamon. Mix well without beating. Turn into the prepared tin and bake for 1¼ hours until a skewer comes out clean. Remove from the oven and leave to cool in the tin. When cold, turn out and serve with the pineapple side uppermost.

Threshing Cake

Threshing time was the most important time of the farming calendar when the grain was gathered in and stored for use during the winter. The 15 to 20 extra workers had to be fed and this cake helped to satisfy their hunger during the afternoon break. Many areas of Britain had their own dishes for threshing time, and this fruit loaf was a Welsh speciality.

100g (4oz) dripping or lard
225g (8oz) plain flour, sifted
100g (4oz) caster sugar
225g (8oz) mixed dried fruit
1 egg, beaten
¼ teaspoon bicarbonate of soda dissolved
**   in 1 tablespoon buttermilk or sour milk**
A little extra buttermilk or sour milk

Makes 1 x 900g (2lb) loaf

Preheat the oven to 190°C, 375°F, gas mark 5. Grease and line a 900g (2lb) loaf tin. Rub the fat into the flour. Add the sugar and dried fruit and stir well. Add the beaten egg and bicarbonate of soda and mix with enough buttermilk or sour milk to give a soft consistency. Turn into the prepared tin and bake for 1½ hours until a skewer comes out clean. Remove from the oven and turn on to a wire rack to cool.

Welsh Honey and Ginger Cake

In Wales, tea was always a very popular meal on Sundays and special occasions. Most Welsh homes used to rely on a bakestone for making bread but a makeshift oven could be made by upturning a large iron cooking pot over the bakestone. In some homes, a baking oven was built into the fireplace so that cakes like this could be cooked ready for tea.

100g (4oz) butter
225g (8oz) clear honey
150ml (5fl oz) milk
450g (1lb) plain flour, sifted
Pinch of salt
2½ teaspoons baking powder
3 teaspoons ground ginger
100g (4oz) sultanas
50g (2oz) mixed candied peel
2 eggs, beaten

Makes 1 x 20cm (8in) round cake

Preheat the oven to 180°C, 350°F, gas mark 4. Grease and line a 20cm (8in) round tin. Melt the butter gently with the honey and milk. Remove from the heat and leave to cool. Mix together the flour, salt, baking powder, ginger and dried fruit. Add the beaten eggs and the butter mixture and mix to a soft consistency. Turn into the prepared tin and bake for 1¼–1½ hours until a skewer comes out clean. (Check the top after half an hour and, if it is beginning to brown too much, cover with a double layer of greaseproof paper.) Remove from the oven and turn out on to a wire rack to cool.

Welsh Lardy Cake

Lardy cake was made to use up some of the fat left over from the family pig after the annual slaughter. Most rural families kept at least one pig, fattening it up on all the waste food during the year and then killing it in the autumn to provide food during the winter. Nothing was wasted – bacon, ham, fresh and salt pork provided joints of meat, trotters were used for brawn, the head was boiled to make a strong jelly stock, the cheeks were made into 'Bath chaps', the offal went into black pudding, dripping was spread on bread and toast, and the lard was used for frying and for making pastry, puddings and lardy cakes.

15g (½oz) fresh yeast (to substitute dried yeast, see page 11)

1 tablespoon caster sugar

300ml (10fl oz) warm water

450g (1lb) plain flour, sifted

1 teaspoon salt

225g (8oz) lard, softened

100g (4oz) currants

50g (2oz) mixed candied peel

50g (2oz) caster or granulated sugar

A little extra plain flour

Makes 9 generous pieces

Cream together the yeast and caster sugar and mix with the warm water. Mix together the flour and salt, add the yeast mixture and mix to a soft dough. Knead for 3–4 minutes, then put in a bowl and leave in a warm place for 1–1½ hours until doubled in size. Preheat the oven to 200°C, 400°F, gas mark 6. Grease a 22.5cm (9in) square tin. On a floured board, roll out the dough to a thickness of 1cm (½in). Divide the lard, currants, peel and sugar into four equal portions. Spread a quarter of the lard on the dough and sprinkle over a quarter of the currants, peel and sugar and a little flour. Fold the dough in half and repeat the rolling, dotting and folding process three more times until all the ingredients are used. Place the folded dough in the prepared tin and bake for 25–30 minutes until golden brown. Remove from the oven and leave to cool in the tin. When cold, cut into squares and lift out of the tin. To serve, warm in the oven or microwave.

Pratie Cake

Like so many Irish recipes, this cake relies on potatoes but adds apples, brown sugar and butter to create a juicy, fruity, double-layer, pie-like treat. It is best served hot straight from the oven with a strong cup of Irish breakfast blend or a strong Assam or Ceylon tea.

450g (1lb) potatoes, boiled and mashed
1 teaspoon salt
50g (2oz) butter, melted
4 tablespoons plain flour, sifted
4–6 cooking apples, peeled, cored and sliced
2 tablespoons demerara or light soft brown sugar
A little milk
25–50g (1–2oz) butter
Demerara or caster sugar for dredging

Makes 1 x 17.5cm (7in) round cake

Preheat the oven to 190°C, 375°F, gas mark 5. Grease a baking tray. Mix together the mashed potatoes, salt and butter and work in the flour to give a pliable dough. Knead lightly, then divide into two portions. On a floured board, roll each piece out into a round approximately 17.5cm (7in) in diameter, making one slightly larger than the other. Place the larger round on the baking tray and lay the apple slices on top of the dough. Sprinkle with the sugar. Dampen the edges of the dough with a little milk and lay the other round on top. Press the edges well together. Bake for 45–60 minutes until the apples are tender and the top is golden. Remove from the oven, spread with butter, dredge all over with sugar and serve hot.

If liked, add half a teaspoon of ground ginger to the mixture with the flour, and, if you prefer a sweeter cake, also add a little caster sugar.

Walsingham Honey Cake

Little Walsingham became an important place of pilgrimage when visions of the Virgin Mary were seen there, and the area has also long been famous for its bees and honey. Honey has for centuries been used to treat wounds and it is known today that it does indeed have an antibacterial effect and therefore helps the body to heal.

FOR THE CAKE
225g (8oz) butter, softened
225g (8oz) light soft brown sugar
2 eggs, beaten
450g (1lb) plain flour, sifted
1 teaspoon ground ginger
1 teaspoon bicarbonate of soda
100g (4oz) raisins
50g (2oz) mixed candied peel
50g (2oz) glacé cherries, halved
300ml (10fl oz) milk
75g (3oz) clear honey
75g (3oz) black treacle

FOR THE TOPPING
3-4 tablespoons clear honey
40g (1½oz) light soft brown sugar
50g (2oz) butter
50g (2oz) flaked almonds

Makes 1 x 17.5cm (7in) square cake

Preheat the oven to 160°C, 325°F, gas mark 3. Grease and line a 17.5cm (7in) square tin. Beat together the butter and sugar until light and fluffy. Add the beaten eggs and beat again. Add the flour, ginger and bicarbonate of soda and beat well. Stir in the dried fruit and cherries. Warm together the milk, honey and treacle and add gradually, beating well and making sure that all the ingredients are evenly distributed. Turn into the prepared tin and bake for 2 hours until a skewer comes out clean. Remove from the oven and leave in the tin. Warm together the honey, sugar and butter and pour over the warm cake. Sprinkle with the almonds and allow to cool completely in the tin.

Banbury Cakes

Banbury cakes date back to pagan days and are thought to have been eaten at May Day celebrations. Recipes have changed greatly over the centuries, varying from a type of fruited bread flavoured with caraway seeds, to pastry cases filled with fruit, saffron and sherry. Today's cakes are a fruit-filled pastry with a flaky outer case and plump dried fruit inside.

350g (12oz) puff pastry (see page 14)
50g (2oz) butter
100g (4oz) currants
50g (2oz) mixed candied peel
¼ teaspoon ground cinnamon
½ teaspoon allspice or grated nutmeg
25g (1oz) light or dark soft brown sugar
1 tablespoon dark rum
A little milk or water
1 egg white, lightly beaten
Caster sugar for dredging

Makes 11–12 cakes

Make the pastry according to the instructions on page 14 and chill for at least 30 minutes. Melt the butter in a small pan and add the dried fruit, spices, brown sugar and rum. Stir and leave to cool. Preheat the oven to 230°C, 450°F, gas mark 8. Grease two baking trays. On a lightly floured board, roll out the pastry to a thickness of 0.5cm (¼in) and cut into rounds approximately 10cm (4in) in diameter. Place a spoonful of the fruit mixture on each circle, dampen the edges of the pastry with a little milk or water and gather the edges together. Seal well, turn each cake over and roll gently to a neat oval shape. Cut three slashes in the top and place on prepared trays. Brush the tops with the beaten egg white and dredge with caster sugar. Bake for 10–15 minutes until golden. Remove from oven and lift on to a wire rack to cool slightly before serving.

Welsh Cakes

The most famous of traditional cakes from Wales, these little flat spicy griddle cakes were offered to visitors calling at the house. Welsh cakes were traditionally cooked on a bakestone that sat on the open kitchen fire. Their name in Welsh is pice ary maen *which literally means 'cakes on the stone'. Two variations are cooked today – Llech Cymreig is made with plain flour to give a flatter, crisper cake, and Jam Split is made by cutting the Welsh cake across the middle and filling it with jam.*

225g (8oz) self-raising flour, sifted
Pinch of salt
50g (2oz) lard, softened
50g (2oz) butter, softened
75g (3oz) granulated sugar
25g (1oz) currants
½ egg, beaten
1½ tablespoons milk
Caster sugar for sprinkling

Makes 10–12 cakes

Preheat a griddle or a heavy frying pan to a moderate, even temperature. Mix together the flour and salt and rub in the fat. Add the sugar and currants and mix with the egg and milk to a soft dough. On a floured board, roll out to a thickness of 0.5–1cm (¼–½in) and cut out rounds using a 7.5cm (3in) cutter. Place on the griddle and cook both sides until light golden. Lift on to a wire rack to cool and sprinkle with caster sugar before serving.

Right: Welsh Cakes
Next page: Walsingham Honey Cake

Daniel's Coffee and Drambuie Meringues

This luxurious recipe comes from Fountains Abbey and Studley Royal which boasts a beautiful naturalistic park that surrounds the Abbey. The Banqueting House was originally intended for the consumption of sweetmeats, fruit and sweet wines after dinner, but during the 18th century buildings like this were more frequently used as a venue for a tea party. In the basement there was often a little scullery and a pantry where the maid could prepare the foods and store the teawares. These meringues are impressive enough to be served as a dessert at a dinner party or at a special tea party.

4 egg whites
225g (8oz) caster sugar
1 teaspoon cornflour
1 teaspoon vanilla essence
½ teaspoon white wine vinegar
300ml (10fl oz) double cream, whipped
3 tablespoons Drambuie
1 teaspoon finely ground coffee
8 walnut halves

Makes 8 meringue nests

Preheat the oven to 110°C, 225°F, gas mark ¼. Cover a baking tray with greaseproof paper. Whisk the egg whites with 100g (4oz) of the sugar until very stiff. Add another 100g (4oz) of sugar and whisk again. Add the cornflour, vanilla essence and vinegar and fold carefully in. Place the mixture in a large piping bag fitted with a 1cm (½in) star nozzle and pipe eight nests on to the greaseproof paper. Bake for 1 hour, then reduce the oven temperature to the lowest possible setting and bake for 4 hours more. Remove from the oven and leave to cool. If not needed immediately, place in an airtight container. When ready to use, mix together the whipped cream, Drambuie and coffee and place in a piping bag. Pipe the cream into the nests and decorate each with a half walnut.

Left: Daniel's Coffee and Drambuie Meringues
Previous page: Banbury Cakes

Cheshire Souling Cakes

Souling cakes were baked for All Souls' Day when children went around the villages begging for sustenance. The cakes are thought to have descended from the food that was left out in graves for the dead in pagan days.

350g (12oz) plain flour, sifted
½ teaspoon ground cinnamon
½ teaspoon mixed spice
Pinch of nutmeg
175g (6oz) caster sugar
175g (6oz) butter, softened
1 egg, beaten
1½ teaspoons white wine vinegar

Makes approximately 26 cakes

Preheat the oven to 180°C, 350°F, gas mark 4. Grease two baking trays. Mix together all the dry ingredients and rub in the butter. Add the beaten egg and vinegar and mix to a soft dough. Knead gently until smooth. On a lightly floured board, roll out to a thickness of 0.5cm (¼in) and cut into rounds with a 7.5cm (3in) cutter. Place on the prepared trays and bake for 15–20 minutes until lightly browned. Remove from the oven and leave to cool on the trays for a few minutes before lifting carefully on to a wire rack to cool completely.

Eccles Cakes

Over the centuries, several regions of Britain developed their own versions of this fruit-filled pastry. Oxfordshire's Banbury Cakes are famous while, in Coventry, God Cakes were triangular to represent the Holy Trinity. Eccles cakes are thought to be descendants of cakes and loaves made as an offering at pagan and early Christian festivals.

225–275g (8–10oz) flaky pastry (see page 14)
25g (1oz) butter, softened
25g (1oz) light soft brown sugar
25g (1oz) mixed candied peel
75g (3oz) currants
1 teaspoon mixed spice
A little milk or water
1 egg white, beaten
2 tablespoons caster sugar

Makes 12 cakes

Make the pastry according to the instructions on page 14 and chill for at least 1 hour. Grease two baking trays. On a floured board, roll out the pastry to a thickness of approximately 0.5cm (¼in) and cut out circles using a 10cm (4in) cutter (a cup or bowl will do very nicely if you do not have a big enough cutter). Mix together the butter and brown sugar, add the dried fruit and spice and mix well. Place a teaspoonful of the mixture on each pastry circle. Dampen the edges of the pastry with a little milk or water, gather the edges together and seal well. Turn the cakes over so that the joins are underneath. Roll each one out so that the currants just show through the pastry and place on the prepared trays. Chill for 10–15 minutes. Meanwhile heat the oven to 230°C, 450°F, gas mark 8. Make two or three slits on the top of each cake, brush with beaten egg white and dredge with caster sugar. Bake for 10–15 minutes until crisp and golden. Remove from the oven and lift carefully on to a wire rack to cool.

Suffolk Cakes

These light buttery biscuits are perfect with a cup of tea at any time of the day. When pairing different teas to different foods, choose lighter teas to suit lighter foods and stronger, more robust teas to drink with strong flavours such as beef, cheese, rich creamy cakes and chocolate. With fish, Japanese, Thai and Chinese foods, drink a green tea. White teas and oolongs are often so wonderfully light and aromatic, they are best drunk alone.

2 eggs, separated
100g (4oz) caster sugar
Grated rind of half a lemon
50g (2oz) butter, softened
50g (2oz) plain flour, sifted

Makes 10 buns

Preheat the oven to 200°C, 400°F, gas mark 6. Place paper cases in ten patty tins. Beat the egg whites until very stiff. Beat the egg yolks and add to the whites with the sugar, lemon rind and butter. Beat well. Fold in the flour and spoon the mixture into the paper cases. Bake for 10–15 minutes until pale golden and firm. Remove from the oven and lift on to a wire rack to cool.

Fat Rascals

These fruity buns with their rich brown crust are said to come originally from the Cleveland area between County Durham and Yorkshire. Thought to date back to the mid-19th century, they go well with a strong cup of Yorkshire tea.

225g (8oz) plain flour, sifted
Pinch of salt
100g (4oz) butter, softened
40g (1½oz) caster sugar
50g (2oz) currants
50–75ml (2–3fl oz) milk and water, mixed
Caster sugar for dredging

Makes 7–8 biscuits

Preheat the oven to 200°C, 400°F, gas mark 6. Grease a baking tray. Mix together the flour and salt and rub in the butter. Add the sugar and currants and mix. Add enough milk and water to give a firm dough. On a floured board, roll out to a thickness of 1cm (½in) and cut out circles using a 7.5cm (3in) cutter. Place on the prepared tray, dredge with caster sugar and bake for 20–25 minutes until pale golden. Remove from the oven and lift carefully on to a wire rack to cool.

Chocolate Truffle Cake

This is named after the soft, velvety smooth confectionery that originated in France. The ganache centre of a truffle is made of solid chocolate and cream and is often flavoured with vanilla, brandy or rum. The name probably comes from the similarity in appearance between a chocolate truffle and the small, dark fungus so highly prized in France.

675g (1½lb) left-over cake (any sort), broken into small pieces
100g (4oz) jam (any sort)
50g (2oz) mixed, unsalted nuts, roughly chopped
50g (2oz) cocoa powder, sifted
3–4 tablespoons orange juice
225–275g (8–10oz) milk or plain chocolate
50g (2oz) blanched, split almonds, toasted

Makes 9 pieces

Grease and line a 17.5cm (7in) square tin. Mix together the cake, jam, nuts, cocoa powder and enough orange juice to bind the mixture. Press into the prepared tin and smooth the top. Melt the chocolate and pour over the surface. Spread evenly and sprinkle with the almonds. Place in the refrigerator to set. When set, cut into pieces and lift carefully out of the tin.

This is an excellent and quick way to turn left-over cake into a rich, delicious chocolate treat.

Florentine Slice

This rich, chocolate slice is made to a recipe from Kingston Lacy in Dorset, once the home of the Bankes family. Margaret Bankes, who lived there in the 17th and 18th century, began buying teaware for the house and between 1701 and 1710, she acquired various 'setts of tea dishes and saucers', 'a kenester' , 'a china sugar dish', a pair of tea tongs and 10 teapots. She also purchased 'a black Japan table for my closet' (where she took tea) and four more tea tables.

350g (12oz) good quality milk or plain chocolate
350g (12oz) mixed dried fruit (raisins, sultanas, currants, peel)
100g (4oz) glacé cherries
100g (4oz) shredded coconut
100g (4oz) caster sugar
50g (2oz) butter, melted
2 eggs, beaten

Makes 16 slices

Line a 20 x 27.5cm (8 x 11in) tin with foil. Melt the chocolate and spread evenly in the base of the tin. Leave to cool in the refrigerator until set. Preheat the oven to 180°C, 350°F, gas mark 4. Mix together the dried fruit, glacé cherries, coconut, sugar, butter and beaten eggs and spread evenly over the chocolate. Bake for 25 minutes until golden brown. Remove from the oven and leave to cool in the tin. When cool, place the tin in the refrigerator until really cold. Cut into fingers and turn out of the tin.

This rich, gooey cake contains no flour, so is ideal for people who cannot eat wheat.

Ginger Flapjack

The name 'flapjack' seems to have started life in North America as a pancake but evolved somewhere along the line into a flat, oaty confectionery. Usually made with oats rather than flour, they are a good option for anyone who cannot eat wheat.

FOR THE FLAPJACK
175g (6oz) butter
25g (1oz) golden syrup
100g (4oz) light soft brown sugar
225g (8oz) porridge oats
50g (2oz) shredded coconut
1 teaspoon ground ginger

FOR THE TOPPING
175–225g (6–8oz) icing sugar, sifted
1 teaspoon ground ginger
1–2 tablespoons cold water

Makes 10–12 pieces

Preheat the oven to 180°C, 350°F, gas mark 4. Grease a 17.5 x 27.5cm (7 x 11in) Swiss roll tin. Melt together the butter, syrup and sugar. Stir in the oats, coconut and ginger and mix well. Turn into the prepared tin and bake for 20 minutes until golden and firm. Remove from the oven and leave to cool in the tin. When cold, prepare the topping by mixing together the icing sugar, ginger and water. Spread the icing over the flapjack and leave to set. Cut into pieces and lift carefully from the tin.

Apricot Almond Shortcake

A delicious combination of almonds and apricots, this goes well with a golden Ceylon tea. Ceylon tea is often marketed as Orange Pekoe, which causes confusion as the name has nothing to do with orange flavouring or the colour of the leaves. Today Orange Pekoe (OP) is used as a grading term for tea denoting the size and appearance of the leaf but the origins are more complicated. When the Dutch started importing tea to Europe it was so expensive that only the Royal family, the House of Orange and other wealthy aristocrats, could afford to buy it so the royal name became associated with tea. Pekoe is a Chinese word that refers to the fine downy hairs on the underside of the leaves, known in French as the 'duvet'.

225g (8oz) butter, softened
450g (1lb) self-raising flour, sifted
225g (8oz) caster sugar
2 eggs, beaten
2 teaspoons lemon juice
275g (10oz) ready-to-use dried apricots, roughly chopped
1 egg white, lightly beaten
50g (2oz) flaked almonds

Makes 1 x 22.5cm (9in) round cake

Preheat the oven to 160°C, 325°F, gas mark 3. Grease a 22.5cm (9in) loose-bottomed round shallow flan tin. Rub the butter into the flour and stir in the sugar. Add the eggs and lemon juice and mix to a firm dough. Divide into two portions. On a piece of cling film, roll out half the dough to make a circle to fit the prepared tin. Invert so that the dough rests in the tin, remove the cling film and press the dough down into the tin so that it lines the base and sides. Spread the chopped apricots over the dough. On a piece of cling film, roll out the remaining half of the dough to make a circle to fit the top and invert on to the apricots. Press the edges well together, brush the top with the beaten egg white and sprinkle with the flaked almonds. Bake for 45 minutes to 1 hour until golden. Remove from the oven and leave to cool in the tin. When cold, remove from the tin and cut into portions.

Box Hill Bread Pudding

Bread puddings, popular since the 1300s and a real favourite in the 1940s and 50s, was the cook's way of using up stale bread and so it was often called 'poor man's pudding'. Dried fruits, spices, sugar, eggs and milk were added to soften the dry dough and make it more palatable. Other ways of using up leftover bread was to make bread and butter pudding or Queen of Puddings, a soft, rather sloppy mix of bread and milk, a layer of jam and a frothy meringue topping.

450g (1lb) bread (white, brown or a mixture)
225g (8oz) raisins or currants
100g (4oz) glacé cherries, cut in halves
100g (4oz) shredded suet
100g (4oz) caster sugar
2 teaspoons grated nutmeg
1 teaspoon ground cinnamon
2 eggs, beaten
Milk for mixing

Makes 16 slabs

Break the bread into small pieces, cover with cold water and leave to soak for at least 1 hour. Preheat the oven to 160°C, 325°F, gas mark 3. Grease a shallow baking tin approximately 20 x 30cm (8 x 12in). Strain and squeeze as much water as possible out of the bread and beat to break up any lumps. Add the dried fruit, cherries, suet, sugar, spices and eggs and beat together, adding enough milk to give a soft, dropping consistency. Pour into the prepared tin and bake for 1½–2 hours until firm. Remove from the oven and leave to cool in the tin. When cold, cut into slabs. This traditional cake is adapted from Mrs Beeton's original recipe.

Petworth Pudding

This recipe was found in the archives of Petworth House in Sussex, although it cannot be very old as the ingredients include digestive biscuits which date back to the 1920s. As this has all the richness of dark chocolate, choose a strong Kenyan or China Yunnan tea to drink with it.

100g (4oz) butter
100g (4oz) granulated or caster sugar
25g (1oz) cocoa powder, sifted
1 egg
225g (8oz) digestive biscuits, crushed
50g (2oz) raisins or sultanas
50g (2oz) dark chocolate
50g (2oz) walnuts, chopped, or 50g (2oz) shredded coconut
50g (2oz) glacé cherries, roughly chopped

Makes 16 fingers

Grease a 17.5 x 27.5cm (7x 11in) Swiss roll tin. Melt the butter and sugar in a medium-sized pan. Beat in the cocoa powder and the egg. Stir in the crushed biscuits and raisins or sultanas and turn into the prepared tin. Press down well and smooth the top with a palette knife. Melt the chocolate and pour over the top. Mix together the walnuts or coconut and cherries and sprinkle over the chocolate. Place the tin in the refrigerator and leave to set. When cold, cut into fingers.

Applecake Fingers

Made with local apples, this is an easy recipe from Anglesey Abbey in Cambridgeshire. In the house, there is an interesting piece of Ming porcelain that started life as a ginger jar and was later converted into a teapot. It stands about 17.5cm (7in) tall, is made of brown clay slipware decorated with a cream-coloured design on each side. A delicate silver spout and handle have been added, a silver cherub stands on top of the lid and the jar sits on a fine silver mount. The pot is Chinese and the silver additions would have been fashioned and fitted in Europe.

FOR THE CAKE
150g (5oz) plain flour, sifted
150g (5oz) sugar
½ teaspoon baking powder
½ teaspoon mixed spice
Pinch of salt
90g (3½oz) butter, softened
1 large egg, beaten
75ml (3fl oz) milk
65g (2½oz) cooking or eating apples, chopped

FOR THE GLAZE
175–225g (6–8oz) icing sugar, sifted
1½–2 tablespoons water
A few drops of lemon juice and a little grated lemon rind (optional)

Makes 15 pieces

Preheat the oven to 190°C, 375°F, gas mark 5. Grease a 17.5 x 27.5cm (7 x 11in) Swiss roll tin. Mix together the flour, sugar, baking powder, spice and salt and rub in the butter until the mixture resembles fine breadcrumbs. Add the beaten egg and milk and mix until smooth. Add the chopped apple and mix so that it is evenly distributed. Press into the prepared tin and bake for approximately 35 minutes until golden and firm. Remove from the oven and leave to cool in the tin. When cold, mix together the icing sugar, water, lemon juice and rind if using, and pour the icing over the top of the cake. Leave to set, then cut the cake into fingers and lift carefully from the tin.

Paradise Slice

The semolina in this mixture adds to the interesting variety of textures and flavours. Semolina is made by milling wheat or maize. It is unusual to include it in this type of cake and the coarse grains are more normally boiled in milk with sugar to make a sort of sweet porridge and finely ground versions are used to make pasta and noodles.

175g (6oz) shortcrust pastry (see page 16)
100g (4oz) butter, softened
100g (4oz) caster sugar
1 egg, beaten
50g (2oz) semolina
50g (2oz) shredded coconut
50g (2oz) glacé cherries, chopped
50g (2oz) walnuts, chopped
175g (6oz) sultanas

Makes 10 slices

Make the pastry according to the instructions on page 16 and chill for at least 15 minutes. Preheat the oven to 190°C, 375°F, gas mark 5. Grease a 17.5 x 27.5cm (7 x 11in) Swiss roll tin. On a lightly floured board, roll out the pastry and use to line the prepared tin. Beat together the butter and sugar until light and fluffy. Add the egg and beat again. Add the remaining ingredients and mix thoroughly. Turn into the pastry case and smooth. Bake for 20–25 minutes until golden and firm. Remove from the oven and leave to cool in the tin. When cold, cut into pieces and lift carefully from the tin.

Date and Oat Slices

Teatime menus today often include cakes that offer a slightly healthier option and are not so high in calories. We do now believe that tea helps to reduce cholesterol and keep our arteries functioning properly so a cup of tea with a slice of this cake is a good teatime choice.

225g (8oz) dates, roughly chopped
75g (3oz) shredded coconut
75g (3oz) porridge oats
75g (3oz) plain wholemeal flour, sifted
40g (1½oz) light soft brown sugar
¾ teaspoon baking powder
175g (6oz) butter, softened
Demerara sugar for sprinkling

Makes 15 squares

Preheat the oven to 180°C, 350°F, gas mark 4. Grease a 17.5 x 27.5cm (7 x 11in) Swiss roll tin. Cover the dates with water and simmer until soft. Mix together the dry ingredients and rub in the butter to form a crumbly mixture. Sprinkle half the mixture into the prepared tin and press down lightly. Spread the softened dates over the base and add the remaining crumbly mixture. Spread evenly, press down lightly and sprinkle liberally with demerara sugar. Bake for 25–30 minutes until browned. Remove from the oven, leave to cool in the tin and then cut into squares.

Apricot Swiss Roll

Apricots and almonds go exceptionally well together in this luxury, creamy rolled sponge. To eat this without ending up with very sticky fingers, little tea knives or pastry forks are needed. In the Edwardian period, the heyday for tea, several new pieces of tea equipage were developed, including sets of pastry forks, tea knives, muffin dishes for keeping buttered muffins and crumpets hot, and muffineers, invented for shaking cinnamon sugar on to buttered toast.

FOR THE SPONGE
2 eggs
75g (3oz) caster sugar
75g (3oz) self-raising flour, sifted
Caster sugar for dusting

FOR THE FILLING
1 x 410g (14½oz) tin apricots, drained and the juice reserved
1–2 tablespoons brandy
150ml (5fl oz) whipped cream
25g (1oz) flaked almonds, untoasted
25g (1oz) flaked almonds, toasted
Icing sugar for dusting

Serves 6

To make the sponge, preheat the oven to 160°C, 325°F, gas mark 3. Grease and line a 17.5 x 27.5cm (7x 11in) Swiss roll tin. Beat the eggs thoroughly. Add the sugar and continue beating until thick and mousse-like. Fold in the flour and turn into the prepared tin. Bake for 10–15 minutes until the sponge springs back when lightly pressed. Remove from the oven and invert the tin on to a clean teacloth dusted with a little caster sugar. Roll the sponge immediately round a wooden rolling pin or a milk bottle and leave to cool. Meanwhile slice the apricots and soak in the brandy. Just before serving, carefully unroll the sponge and spread with the whipped cream. Arrange the apricots over the top and pour on the brandy. Sprinkle with the untoasted almonds and carefully roll the sponge up again. Place on a serving dish, pour a little of the reserved apricot juice over the sponge, sprinkle the top with toasted almonds and dust with icing sugar. Serve immediately.

This makes a mouthwatering dessert or a very special cake for tea.

Sweetmince Squares

Filled with a sort of mincemeat mixture, this Irish recipe includes cinnamon and ginger. Under the rule of the Portuguese and then the Dutch, the island of Sri Lanka was once the world's main producer of cinnamon. Ginger has all sorts of health benefits. It can help ease nausea, reduce inflammation, settle the digestion, and minimise pain from arthritis. Both spices are also commonly used as additional flavourings for tea, added to the tea after it has been manufactured. Flavoured teas are becoming more and more popular among younger consumers who love the flower petals and pieces of fruit that are often added for visual effect.

675g (1½lb) rich shortcrust pastry (see page 15)

1½ teaspoons cornflour

½ teaspoon custard powder

175ml (6fl oz) water

175g (6oz) currants and raisins

50g (2oz) mixed candied peel

75g (3oz) caster, granulated or demerara sugar

1 teaspoon ground cinnamon

1 teaspoon mixed spice

½ teaspoon ground ginger

A little water or milk

Caster sugar for dredging

Makes 15 squares

Make the pastry according to the instructions on page 15 and chill for at least 15 minutes. Preheat the oven to 180°C, 350°F, gas mark 4. Grease a 17.5 x 27.5cm (7 x 11in) Swiss roll tin. On a floured board, roll out half the pastry and use to line the prepared tin. Mix together the cornflour and custard powder with the water and put with all the other ingredients for the filling into a pan. Bring to the boil and simmer until thick. Turn into the pastry case and spread evenly. Roll out the remaining pastry and lay on top. Wet the edges of the pastry with a little water or milk and press well together. Bake for 45–50 minutes until golden. Remove from the oven and dredge with caster sugar. Allow to cool in the tin. When cold, cut into squares.

Right: Sweetmince Squares
Next page: Apricot Swiss Roll

Apricot Sesame Slice

As well as adding their distinctive flavour and aroma to foods, sesame seeds are rich in minerals and vitamins and also have antioxidant properties. They marry very well with the apricots in this recipe.

FOR THE BASE
100g (4oz) butter
100g (4oz) golden syrup
100g (4oz) demerara sugar
225g (8oz) porridge oats
100g (4oz) shredded coconut
50g (2oz) sesame seeds, untoasted
3 teaspoons ground cinnamon
Pinch of salt
100g (4oz) dried apricots, roughly chopped
100g (4oz) chocolate chips (milk or plain)

FOR THE TOPPING
25g (1oz) sesame seeds, untoasted

Makes 12 slices

Preheat the oven to 150°C, 300°F, gas mark 2. Grease a 20 x 27.5cm (8 x 11in) tin. Melt the butter and syrup together in a large pan. Add the sugar, oats, coconut, sesame seeds, cinnamon, salt and apricots and stir well, making sure that all the ingredients are evenly distributed. Stir in the chocolate chips and mix thoroughly. Turn into the prepared tin and press well down. Smooth the top and sprinkle with the 25g (1oz) sesame seeds. Press well into the mixture and bake for 30–35 minutes until golden and firm. Remove from the oven and leave to cool in the tin. When cold, cut into slices or squares.

Left: Apricot Sesame Slice
Previous page: Flapjack

Flapjack

Oats were always considered to be an inferior food that was often fed to horses. In his dictionary, Samuel Johnson described oats as 'a grain, which in England is generally given to horses, but in Scotland supports the people'. Today we recognize the health benefits of including fibre (good for our heart) and protein in our diet.

100g (4oz) butter
6 tablespoons golden syrup
75g (3oz) self-raising wholemeal
225g (8oz) rolled oats

Makes 12 pieces

Preheat the oven to 160°C, 325°F, gas mark 3. Grease a shallow 18cm (7½in) square tin. In a medium-sized pan, melt the butter and syrup over a low heat. Remove from the heat and add the oats. Mix thoroughly so that all the ingredients are evenly distributed. Turn into the prepared tin, press down and smooth the top with a palette knife. Bake for 30–40 minutes until golden. Remove from the oven and leave to cool in the tin for 5–10 minutes, then cut into pieces and lift carefully on to a wire rack to finish cooling.

Suffolk Apple Cake

This is a traditional cake from a county that has always been an important apple-growing area of England. And when it's time to brew a pot of tea to go with it, remember that there are thousands of different teas made around the world in more than 35 countries and every single one of them is different. For, although all teas are made from the leaves and leaf buds of the tea bush (the Camellia sinensis*), the bush grows differently in different conditions. Just as different grape varietals give different wine characters, so the different cultivars of the tea bush have their own individual flavour and aroma. And with the huge variey, there is a tea to suit all palates.*

225g (8oz) plain flour, sifted

1½ teaspoons baking powder

Pinch of salt

100g (4oz) lard or dripping

225g (8oz) eating apples (weighed after being
    peeled and cored), finely chopped or grated

1½ tablespoons caster, granulated or demerara sugar

1-2 tablespoons milk

Makes 1 x 20cm (8in) round cake

Preheat the oven to 180°C, 350°F, gas mark 4. Grease a baking tray. Mix together the flour, baking powder and salt and rub in the fat. Add the apples, sugar and enough milk to give a soft dough. Place the dough on the prepared tray and shape with the hands into a flat round cake approximately 20cm (8in) across and 1–1.5cm (½–¾in) thick. Bake for 40–45 minutes until golden and firm. Remove from the oven and serve hot, split and buttered.

Toffee Bars

*What could be more fun than going out to tea at one of the National Trust tearooms
and enjoying something sweet and sticky like these cakes? The idea of tearooms started in
Glasgow and spread to London when a well-known bread company called the ABC (the
Aerated Bread Company) decided to turn a spare back room at their London Bridge branch
into a public tearoom. Their success prompted other companies to open their own tearooms
and soon all of Britain was enjoying 'going out to tea'. The National Trust tearooms always
offer a very welcome chance to sit for a while over a refreshing pot of tea and something
delicious to eat.*

FOR THE CAKE
100g (4oz) butter, softened
100g (4oz) light soft brown sugar
1 egg yolk
50g (2oz) plain flour, sifted
50g (2oz) porridge oats

FOR THE TOPPING
75g (3oz) plain chocolate
25g (1oz) butter
50g (2oz) walnuts or almonds, chopped

Makes 12 bars

Preheat the oven to 190°C, 375°F, gas mark 5. Grease a 17.5 x 27.5cm (7 x 11in) Swiss roll tin. Beat
together the butter, sugar and egg yolk until light and smooth. Add the flour and oats and mix well.
Press into the prepared tin and bake for 15–20 minutes until lightly browned. Remove from the
oven and leave to cool slightly in the tin. Melt together the chocolate and butter for the topping and
spread over the cake. Cover with the chopped nuts and leave to set. While still warm, cut into bars
and leave in the tin until completely cold.

Date and Apple Slices

This rich mixture of fresh and dried fruits and nuts comes from Buckland Abbey in Devon. Crunchy, locally grown apples are mixed with dates that in Britain's past were imported from such far away places as North Africa and Arabia. The long, pointed leaves are traditionally used in Palm Sunday Christian celebrations and as part of the traditional rituals at the Jewish holiday of Sukkot (Feast of the Tabernacles).

450g (1lb) Coxes eating apples, with the peel left on, cored and diced
75g (3oz) mixed unsalted nuts, roughly chopped
100g (4oz) stoned dates, roughly chopped
100g (4oz) self-raising flour, sifted
100g (4oz) dark soft brown or demerara sugar
1 tablespoon clear honey
25g (1oz) butter, melted
1 egg, beaten
Pinch of salt

Makes 10–12 slices

Preheat the oven to 200°C, 400°F, gas mark 6. Grease a 17.5 x 27.5cm (7 x 11in) Swiss roll tin. Mix all the ingredients together and beat with a wooden spoon to ensure that they are evenly distributed. Turn into the prepared tin and press flat. Bake for 30 minutes until firm and golden. Remove from the oven and leave to cool in the tin. When cold, cut into slices and lift carefully from the tin.

Index